Creative Activities for Music and Humanities Classes

Gail Underwood Parker

J. Weston WALCH
PUBLISHER

PORTLAND, MAINE

To the joys of my life:

Leah, Miriam, Anna, and Alexis, who overlooked many "make-your-own-dinner" nights and made it possible for me to write.

User's Guide
to
Walch Reproducible Books

As part of our general effort to provide educational materials which are as practical and economical as possible, we have designated this publication a "reproducible book." The designation means that purchase of the book includes purchase of the right to limited reproduction of all pages on which this symbol appears:

Here is the basic Walch policy: We grant to individual purchasers of this book the right to make sufficient copies of reproducible pages for use by all students of a single teacher. This permission is limited to a single teacher, and does not apply to entire schools or school systems, so institutions purchasing the book should pass the permission on to a single teacher. Copying of the book or its parts for resale is prohibited.

Any questions regarding this policy or requests to purchase further reproduction rights should be addressed to:

Permissions Editor
J. Weston Walch, Publisher
321 Valley Street • P. O. Box 658
Portland, Maine 04104-0658

1   2   3   4   5   6   7   8   9   10
ISBN 0-8251-2803-X

CONTENTS

ACKNOWLEDGMENTS

Thank you to—

My parents, James and Ethel Underwood, who raised me to love music, writing, and stretching my mind, and who were the first to encourage me to write . . . Patti Brassard, Margaret Welch, Claire Ramsbotham, Jill Bell, and Bev Bisbee who have provided encouragement and proofreading . . . Roxie Choate, Patti Gordan, and Leslie Chadborne for giving feedback as musicians . . . All the teachers who attended my workshops, tried my materials, and found them useful enough to buy more . . . All the literally thousands of students who inspired me to create activities for music class that would stretch their minds, challenge their ideas, and open their eyes . . . and Richard Kimball for giving me the support that took this from a simple proposal to the book you now hold.

About the Author

Gail Underwood Parker has taught middle school classroom and choral music for almost 20 years. In 1980 she began giving workshops on her methods at state music conventions. By 1985 these workshops had resulted in a variety of short, published materials for music classrooms, workshops in other states, and a role as leading writer of a state project to develop a K–12 music curriculum. Two years later a flexible, practical curriculum was published in workbook format that allowed teachers to evaluate and build their band, chorus, and classroom music programs. A resident of Cape Elizabeth, Maine, since 1970, Ms. Parker now teaches fifth grade and continues as a freelance writer. She enjoys the nearby ocean, photography, community musical theater, and church work. Most of all, Ms. Parker finds joy in her daughters Belinda, Leah, Miriam, Anna, and Alexis.

INTRODUCTION

Music teachers today are faced with a growing list of concerns. Many schools are reducing or eliminating the music program, due to budget concerns. Like all educators, music teachers are expected to teach more and more with less and less time. Schools encourage interdisciplinary teaching, but seldom provide planning time for its creation and nurturing. School systems want students who can go beyond rote learning to understand and use critical thinking skills. Students need to be aware of their own historical and cultural heritage and yet recognize and value the multicultural diversity of our global community. All this in 45 minutes a week or less!

Current educational research emphasizes the importance of both a variety of presentation methods and personal student involvement as key to developing true comprehension and critical thinking. Music teachers can find it difficult to apply some of the newer classroom instructional techniques to their content area. The market is full of resources for classroom teachers but seldom for the specialty areas. Through experience in my own classroom and in hundreds of workshops, I have had success in devising simple, effective ways of applying several teaching models to music content.

The goal of this book is to provide teachers with a wide variety of immediately usable, complete materials that will actively involve their students and lead to new and deeper understanding about music in individual lives and in society. All the directions, worksheets, checklists, and guides are here to involve students in the lives of composers by role-playing chosen experiences, to engage students in musical decisions by simulating real-life situations, and to entice students to explore areas of music they may never have considered.

HOW TO USE THIS BOOK

WHO SHOULD USE THIS BOOK?

This book contains lessons appropriate for middle school, junior high, and high school students. It can be used by a teacher with no personal music skills or a highly skilled musician. These lessons can be part of a general music program, a music appreciation class, or a humanities class. Lessons cover composers, music repertoire, careers, musical values, elements of music, personal music preferences, and music's role in society, past and present. Some are for a single class and take less than 15 minutes. Others can be for an entire school and community, and fill a week or more.

BUT WHAT ABOUT THE CURRICULUM WE ALREADY HAVE?

This is *not* intended to be a complete music curriculum nor to replace your current curriculum. This is to supplement and enrich your music curriculum. The variety of topics and flexibility of materials allow you, the teacher, to pick and choose the material that most closely dovetails with your class level and your preferred curriculum content. Most music teachers have an abundance of resources for listening lessons, singing, and playing. These materials go the next step.

WHERE DO I START?

The scavenger hunts are probably the easiest place to jump in. Interviews come next, though they require students to find someone to interview. Students always seem to love role-play and simulation activities, but I encourage you to start small until you (and they) get the hang of it. Concept attainment lessons are great to try first as fillers, then as fuller lessons. Inductive lessons require students to gather materials ahead of time. Because there is less teacher direction, they often feel uncomfortable at first, but don't give up. When you feel like a more active plan, try an Up and Moving lesson.

Each section contains introductory hints on how that style of lesson might fit in your curriculum, teacher guidelines or model, detailed directions and materials for one or several lessons, outlines and materials for others, and a list of idea starters for more.

How Do I Choose?

The Activity Comparison Chart (pp. 130–131) is an overview of the book's main lessons in alphabetical order. It shows which lessons do not require personal musical skill. These are great for substitute teachers, humanities teachers without music training, or music teachers working with students who have little or no music background. The chart also indicates the format of each lesson, whether students work individually or in cooperative learning groups, the focus of the lesson, and whether it involves the community.

Why So Few lessons on Reading and Playing Music?

There is more to language and literature than simply decoding and encoding words. Likewise, there is more to music than being able to manipulate and understand its written notation. Music classrooms today are filled with a mix of students at very different levels. When music was taught once a week by a specialist, and reinforced daily by the classroom teacher throughout elementary school, it was possible to assume a degree of comfort and understanding with music "reading" by middle school or junior high. No longer. Now we have students who are fluent from years of private piano or other instrumental instruction, sitting next to classmates who may not understand the difference between a half note and a whole note, much less be able to read a melody on a staff!

Last Chance for "Life Skills" Music

Middle or high school music classes are often the last formal music instruction students receive. Few adults regularly read a melody or play an instrument, but all adults choose how much and what music to use for recreation and pleasure. They will be surrounded by music of their choice (or otherwise!) daily. This may be our last chance to help students acquire the skills, the attitudes, and the understandings to be intelligent music consumers and musically enriched adults. The understanding and valuing of music in life, history, and society becomes a *crucial* goal for our curriculum. I hope this book helps you reach that goal through learning, discovery, and fun!

SCAVENGER HUNTS

WHAT?

Part game, part race, and part exploring: Scavenger hunts are frequently student favorites. With these musical hunts you can add a large dose of learning to the mix. All involve locating as many items as possible from a list and documenting each "find." Whether to reward completeness, speed, or just effort is up to you. The learning is in the process, not just the product.

WHEN?

Scavenger hunts and surveys make learning great fun. Prepared ahead, they can be ideal substitute lessons. They can be part of a school-wide activity or a wonderful opportunity to get local coverage and involve the community. They allow students to explore and test common perceptions and stereotypes.

WHY?

Middle school music appreciation students often ask, "Why do we have to study music anyway? I'm not going to be a musician!" Scavenger hunts are excellent vehicles for raising student awareness of the place of music in *everyone's* lives, not just in professional musicians' lives. Students can uncover stereotypes in our world's view of music and musicians. Students discover how wide the influence and variety of music is in the history, recreation, and "soul" of our society and world.

HOW?

Be sure you are prepared and have any necessary information before you send students searching. Decide if this is to be done individually or in cooperative groups. You may wish to personalize the introductory notes or surveys. Try the scavenger hunt yourself! Afterward, adjust the student worksheets as necessary to ensure clarity and student success.

AND THEN?

Consider an interdisciplinary unit built on a scavenger hunt. Work with the math department to tabulate the results and display them with a variety of graphs or tables. On a grander scale, you can involve the writing department as students develop newspaper articles, essays, and editorials (or even proposals for the school board) based on the results.

Teacher Guidelines

DO YOU KNOW THE MUSICAL STAFF?

Always a class favorite, this a great way to begin the year (especially for the first grade-level in your building) and to give students a new view of the staff. You should gather your own data ahead of time, using the staff survey on p. 3. Include bus drivers, custodians, cafeteria workers, secretaries, and aides, not just teachers!

MOVE OVER, BILLBOARD!

Cooperative groups of four or five students explore the diverse music preferences within age groups or grade levels. Great for tabulating results school- or grade-wide.

A MUSICAL WEEK ON THE TOWN

Done over the course of a week, this also can be an excellent assignment over the holidays or when a student is taking a trip.

READ ALL ABOUT IT

Ideal as part of a school-wide activity such as Newspaper in Education Week, this can also be done at home. Let students know what newspaper in your area is appropriate to use and whether you prefer a specific issue.

WHERE CAN I FIND IT?

This can be done in a single class period in the library. If everything is run off, *and the library is prepared*, this is workable for substitutes. Good also with a town library. To help librarians be prepared and to make the lesson go smoothly, you should send a copy of the note on p. 4, along with the list of scavenger hunt items (pp. 10–11), to the librarian ahead of time. Ideally the whole class will spend the class period in the library.

AROUND THE WORLD

Here is an opportunity to introduce students to the issues of cultural diversity in music.

SURVEY SAYS

This gives students a lift as they discover they know vocabulary some adults don't.

HEAR ME ROAR

This can work well as part of an interdisciplinary unit for Women's History Month (March) or just to get a lively class discussion going.

Musical Staff?

Dear Colleagues—

Please answer the following questions and return this form to me. Students will be going on a scavenger hunt to find musicians, past and present, in the school. Please help out by answering their questions and initialing their hunt sheets if requested. Don't be shy! Discovering that music played (and plays) a part in the lives of "real" people is very important.

Thank you!

PAST

1. Did you ever play in a school band or orchestra? _____ orchestra or band? _____ instrument: _____

2. Did you ever play in a rock band? _____
   instrument: _____ band's name _____

3. Did you ever sing in a school chorus or church choir? _____
   which? _____ (circle) soprano alto tenor bass

4. Did you ever sing in a folk group? _____ voice part: _____
   name of group _____

5. Did you ever sing or play in a school musical? _____ sing or play?
   _____ musical: _____

6. Did you ever take piano lessons? _____ number of years: _____

7. Did you listen to radio/records a lot when you were in school? _____
   Name a song you remember/liked: _____
   Name a performer/group you liked: _____

PRESENT

8. Do you play in a band or orchestra? _____ instrument? _____
   where? _____

9. Do you play in a rock band? _____ instrument? _____
   what band? _____

10. Do you sing in a chorus or choir? _____ (circle) soprano alto tenor bass
    where? _____

11. Do you sing or play in local musicals? _____ play or sing? _____
    where? _____ musical(s): _____

12. Do you still play piano? _____

13. Do you listen to radio/tapes/CDs a lot now? _____
    Name a song you like: _____
    Name a performer/group you like: _____

Library Scavenger Hunt

Dear Librarian,

    Attached is a copy of a library scavenger hunt that I would like my students to complete sometime during this marking period. The goal is to make students aware of the wide variety of music resources available in the library. They do not have to sign out any of the resources, just locate them and copy the title, subject, and call number onto their paper.

    I have a few questions:

1. I would like to set up a time when I could bring the class to the library for this lesson. Are there any weeks, days, or times that are impossible for you?

   _____

2. Do you care whether students work individually or in groups?

   _____

3. How far in advance do I need to schedule a specific time for a class to come?

   _____

4. Independent work would be encouraged if a book could be used only once by each class. Would it be okay to have students or groups mark a located book with a stick-it note or piece of paper? _____

   Do you have any suggestions or preferences?

   _____

5. Do you have any specific questions or concerns?

   _____

6. When can we get together to discuss this?

   _____

Thank you for your help and support. I look forward to my students exploring the resources that you have available.

Name _____   Date _____

Do You Know the Musical Staff?

Directions: How many of the following can you find? Have each person put their initials next to their name. Scavenger hunt is due _____.

PAST

1. Find a staff member who played in a school band.
   name: _____ init.: _____ instrument: _____

2. Find a staff member who played in a school orchestra.
   name: _____ init.: _____ instrument: _____

3. Find a staff member who played in a rock band.
   name: _____ init.: _____ instrument: _____

4. Find a staff member who sang in a school chorus.
   name: _____ init.: _____ voice part: _____

5. Find a staff member who sang in a church choir.
   name: _____ init.: _____ voice part: _____

6. Find a staff member who sang in a folk group.
   name: _____ init.: _____ voice part: _____

7. Find a staff member who sang or played in a school musical.
   name: _____ init.: _____ musical: _____

8. Find a staff member who took piano lessons.
   name: _____ init.: _____ how many years? _____

PRESENT

9. Find a staff member who plays in a band or orchestra.
   name: _____ init.: _____ instrument: _____

10. Find a staff member who plays in a rock band.
    name: _____ init.: _____ instrument: _____

11. Find a staff member who sings in a chorus.
    name: _____ init.: _____ voice part: _____

12. Find a staff member who sings in a church choir.
    name: _____ init.: _____ voice part: _____

13. Find a staff member who sings or plays in local musicals.
    name: _____ init.: _____ musical: _____

14. Find a staff member who still plays piano.
    name: _____ init.: _____

Name _____ Date _____

Move Over, *Billboard*!

Directions: Survey seven people in the age or category your group is studying. Have each person sign in at the top after you have written in their answers. Work with your group to tally and prepare to present your "Top Five."

Category: _____

Participant signatures

1. _____
2. _____
3. _____
4. _____
5. _____
6. _____
7. _____

Favorite music performer(s)

1. _____
2. _____
3. _____
4. _____
5. _____
6. _____
7. _____

Favorite song of today

1. _____
2. _____
3. _____
4. _____
5. _____
6. _____
7. _____

Favorite song of the past

1. _____
2. _____
3. _____
4. _____
5. _____
6. _____
7. _____

Favorite music listening time

1. _____
2. _____
3. _____
4. _____
5. _____
6. _____
7. _____

Favorite type of music

1. _____
2. _____
3. _____
4. _____
5. _____
6. _____
7. _____

       Creative Activities for Music and Humanities Classes

Name _____ Date _____

A Musical Week on the Town

Directions: Write down the date, time, and place you hear music in each of these situations. How many did you run into in a week? _____

A. Store with piped-in music _____

_____

B. Medical office with piped-in music _____

_____

C. Business with phone-hold music _____

_____

D. Someone practicing piano _____

_____

E. Someone practicing another instrument _____

_____

F. Someone humming nearby _____

_____

G. Someone singing nearby _____

_____

H. Someone whistling nearby _____

_____

I. Someone playing a radio _____

_____

J. Someone playing a CD or tape _____

_____

K. A band playing _____

_____

L. A chorus or choir singing _____

_____

M. Background music in a movie _____

_____

N. Background music in a TV show _____

_____

O. TV story/show/news item about music _____

_____

(continued)

7   *Creative Activities for Music and Humanities Classes*

A Musical Week on the Town *(continued)*

Looking Back: At the week's end, look back and write the letter(s) of the category/categories which answer these questions.

1. Which ones did you hear most often? _____

2. Which have you heard before, but not this week? _____

3. Which do you think you would hear any week? _____

4. Which do you think you would rarely hear? _____

What If: Explain your opinion in one or two sentences.

How do you think this hunt might have turned out for your parent(s)? Why?

_____
_____
_____
_____
_____
_____
_____
_____
_____

How do you think it might have turned out for someone younger? Why?

_____
_____
_____
_____
_____
_____
_____
_____
_____

Read All About It

How many of these can you find in the newspaper?

Newspaper: _____   Date & Edition: _____

NEWS

Directions: Write the headline and page number on the line. Attach one clipping to the back.

Review of concert or musical _____

Article about musician _____

Article about an upcoming performance _____

SALES

Directions: Write the store name and sale price on the line. Attach one clipping to the back.

Least expensive CD player _____

Least expensive AM/FM radio _____

Least expensive CDs _____

PUBLICITY

Directions: Write the performer, location, and date. Attach one clipping to the back.

Pop concert _____

Classical concert _____

Musical _____

ADS

Directions: Cut and paste a classified ad for each.

Used piano or organ   Other used instrument

Music lessons   Job opening for musician

Name _____ Date _____

Where Can I Find It?

Directions: Check (√) any of the following you find in the library. Try to find at least five specific items from each section. Star (*) their categories and put the title, subject, and call number of each one you find on the lines provided.

AUDIOVISUAL RESOURCES

Equipment		
Record Players _____	Tape recorders _____	CD players _____
CDs _____	Records _____	Tapes _____
Computers _____	Filmstrips _____	Videos _____
Electronic multimedia services _____		
Topics		
New Age _____	Classical _____	Broadway _____
Jazz _____	Pop _____	Rock _____
Performers _____	Folk _____	Music careers _____
History _____	Composers _____	Movie musicals _____
Ethnic _____	Gen. reference _____	

_____
_____
_____
_____
_____
_____
_____
_____
_____
_____
_____
_____
_____
_____

(continued)

Where Can I Find It? *(continued)*

BIOGRAPHIES

Composers		
American _____	African _____	Pop (past) _____
European _____	South American _____	Pop (present) _____
Eastern _____	Classical _____	
Performers		
American _____	African _____	Pop (past) _____
European _____	South American _____	Pop (present) _____
Eastern _____	Classical _____	Child musician _____

_____

_____

_____

_____

_____

OTHER MUSIC BOOKS

Song collections _____	Music best-sellers _____	Trivia _____
How to _____	About a specific song _____	Magazines _____
Fiction involving music _____		
References		
Music Encyclopedia _____	Music Dictionary _____	
History		
Rock _____	Opera _____	Broadway _____
Folk _____	Classical _____	Jazz _____
American _____		
Picture Books		
Instruments _____	Composers _____	

_____

_____

_____

_____

_____

Around the World

Directions: For years, music study focused on European music. More recently, people have recognized the musical contributions of other world cultures. To see how lopsided general knowledge *still* is, ask people you know to name a song, instrument, and composer from each of the cultures below. Fill in their answers, then check reference books to get answers for any lines left empty, and star (*) those answers.

Europe
1. Song _____
2. Musical instrument _____
3. Composer or performer _____

North America
1. Song _____
2. Musical instrument _____
3. Composer or performer _____

South America
1. Song _____
2. Musical instrument _____
3. Composer or performer _____

Australia
1. Song _____
2. Musical instrument _____
3. Composer or performer _____

Africa
1. Song _____
2. Musical instrument _____
3. Composer or performer _____

Asia
1. Song _____
2. Musical instrument _____
3. Composer or performer _____

Extra Credit: In a paragraph on the back, summarize what this project showed you, whether you think the level of awareness it showed is good or bad, and how it might change.

Survey Says

Directions: Below are five commonly used musical terms. Several are also used in general language with the same meaning. Write down the correct meaning of each next to the word. Then ask three people from each age group to define the word. (Music teachers are off-limits!) For each correct answer, put a star (*) on the line for that age group. Write in the best answer you get. Have each person *sign the back*.

Allegro _____

    under 20 _____

    20s–30s _____

    40s–50s _____

    over 50 _____

    best answer: _____

Crescendo _____

    under 20 _____

    20s–30s _____

    40s–50s _____

    over 50 _____

    best answer: _____

Staccato _____

    under 20 _____

    20s–30s _____

    40s–50s _____

    over 50 _____

    best answer: _____

Mezzo Piano _____

    under 20 _____

    20s–30s _____

    40s–50s _____

    over 50 _____

    best answer: _____

A Cappella _____

    under 20 _____

    20s–30s _____

    40s–50s _____

    over 50 _____

    best answer: _____

Name _____ Date _____

Hear Me Roar

Directions: Helen Reddy's "I Am Woman" became an unofficial anthem of the early women's liberation movement. It said " . . . hear me roar in numbers too big to ignore . . ." What is the role of women in music, past and present? What kind of recognition have women received? Explore these questions by completing this scavenger hunt. Then summarize what you found, your reactions, and your opinions on the back of this sheet.

INFORMATION FROM PEOPLE: Try to find people who can help you fill in any of these blanks. Put a check(√) each time a person you ask *cannot* think of an answer. If they *can*, have them initial their answer.

Name a woman composer
—from before 1800: _____
—from 1800–1900: _____
—from before 1950: _____
—living today: _____

Name a woman musical performer
—from before 1800: _____
—from 1800–1900: _____
—from before 1950: _____
—living today: _____

INFORMATION FROM BOOKS: Try to find answers to the same questions in library books or magazines. Put a check(√) each time you try a book but it does *not* have an answer. Write an answer in when you can find one.

Name a woman composer
—from before 1800: _____
—from 1800–1900: _____
—from before 1950: _____
—living today: _____

Name a woman musical performer
—from before 1800: _____
—from 1800–1900: _____
—from before 1950: _____
—living today: _____

MUSIC INTERVIEWS

WHAT?

Each interview allows a student to explore a career connected to music or music in the community, using a framework of questions.

WHEN?

Interview assignments can be done anytime in the school year. If your school has a career fair or career week, you might want to do them at that time. These assignments can be done by a whole class in the same time frame, as an extra credit option, as an assignment to be done "sometime during the term," or even as a substitute assignment for a student who will be out of school for a period of time.

WHY?

Middle school music appreciation students often view music careers only in terms of performance and teaching. They generally fail to realize how many other careers can connect to a love of or interest in music. Some require musical skill and some do not. This project helps students become more aware of the many ways they can include music in their adult lives and at the same time connect with the real world outside school. It gives them the opportunity to compare attitudes and issues in music in people of different decades, occupations, and religions.

HOW?

Be sure you are prepared and have researched some possible places for interviews in your area. If possible, get permission from a variety of people willing to be interviewed by your students. If time is not an issue, allow the class to generate a list of careers to be represented in the interview and to generate possible questions for people in each career. Be sure to allow class time to discuss the student findings and impressions after the interviews. Perhaps you could make this an interdisciplinary project if you got the language arts teacher to lead the students in writing up the findings.

AND THEN?

Depending on student interest and availability of sites and transportation, consider a follow-up field trip for the whole class or some job-shadowing opportunities for individuals or small groups.

Teacher Guidelines

1. Go over the goals of the interview project with your class. Be sure they can explain them clearly to the interviewees.

2. Choose ahead which interview categories you want them to use. Explain to the class each of the options you have selected.

3. Decide whether students should work individually or cooperatively. (For example: A group might choose one interview category, but individuals in the group would choose different variations from the list below. They could then compare differences within that single category.)

4. Hand out and go over the progress checklist (p. 17).

- Explain that one reason students must check the interviewee choice with you is to make sure that no one person is deluged with requests for interviews. (The goal is to involve a cross-section of the community—not to annoy any individual.)

- Discuss the possibility that some people may not have time available or be willing to be interviewed.

- Consider taking a little class time to role-play some interviews and critique them so that students learn effective, polite techniques.

5. Hand out the appropriate interview sheets (pp. 18–25).

SOME ASSIGNMENT VARIATION IDEAS

"J.Q. Public" Speaks—Emphasize the importance of getting opinions from "ordinary" citizens of various backgrounds (age, sex, ethnicities, occupation).

Remember When?—teens in 1930's, 1940's, 1950's, 1960's, 1970's, 1980's, 1990's

Sing Out!—chorus, choirs, soloists, vocalists with a band

Play It Again, Sam—bands, orchestras, combos, jazz, rock

Library Music—school libraries (elementary, middle school, high school, college), community librarians (small town, city)

Radio Disc Jockey—different radio stations, different formats, different size towns, different times of day

Music in Religion—Christian (different Protestants, Catholic), Jewish, Russian Orthodox, Greek, Buddhist, Islamic

Tape Store Manager—different stores, independent vs. chains, small town vs. city

Name _____ Date _____

Student Checklist

Date or check off each step as you complete it. Attach this checklist to the interview report.

Before

_____ Choose person to be interviewed.

_____ Check choice with teacher.

_____ Obtain person's permission.

_____ Make an appointment for the interview.

_____ Jot down on paper other questions you wish to ask.

_____ Dress appropriately.

_____ Be prepared with extra paper and pencils or pens.

During

_____ Introduce yourself and the project.

_____ Thank the person for willingness to participate.

_____ Be polite and attentive. Be brief.

_____ Write answers on extra paper.

_____ Offer to let the person see the finished report.

After

_____ Thank the person by phone or note if possible.

_____ Write up the interview as soon as possible so that nothing is forgotten.

_____ Hand in the interview report with this checklist attached.

Questions or comments on this project: _____

_____

_____

_____

_____

_____

_____

_____

_____

_____

_____

_____

Interview: "J. Q. Public" Speaks

Person Interviewed: _____ Position: <u>"Ordinary" citizen</u>

Full-time occupation: _____ Sex: __ Approx. Age: _____

Do/did you ever sing or play an instrument? (explain) _____

_____

Do you still? (explain) _____

_____

What was the attitude toward music in your family? _____

Do you listen to music for your own pleasure and/or relaxation? _____

_____

How often/where? _____

_____

Do you enjoy classical? _____ folk? _____ pop? _____ rock? _____ jazz? _____

What performers and/or composers do you enjoy? _____

_____

_____

Do you own a radio? _____ record player? _____ television? _____

cassette player? _____ compact disc player? _____ something portable? _____

About how many do you own? tapes_____ records _____ CDs _____

Do you budget a specific amount for music resource purchases each year?

(Explain) _____

What is the music resource you would most like to have that you don't have?

_____

How would your life change without music? _____

_____

_____

If you could change one thing about your involvement in music, what would it

be? _____

_____

Are you for or against album ratings? _____ single play recordings? _____

background music in stores? _____ in offices? _____ elevators? _____

on-hold phone music? _____ New Age music? _____ music videos? _____

What is your biggest music pet peeve? _____

Interview: Remember When?

Person Interviewed: _____ <u>Teenager</u> in the 19__0's

Name some of the first songs you remember liking as a teenager.

_____

_____

_____

Approximately how much did it cost for a single music recording? _____

Approximately how many did you own as a teenager? _____

Was that typical in your circle of friends? _____

Who were some of the singers/groups you liked to listen to in your teens?

_____

_____

_____

Who were some of the singers/groups your parents liked to listen to?

_____

_____

_____

Did your family own a radio? _____ record player? _____ television? _____

tape player? _____ cassette player? _____ compact disc player? _____

Did you own your own radio? _____ record player? _____ television? _____

tape player? _____ cassette player? _____ compact disc player? _____

How often did you listen to music as a teenager? _____

_____

How often did your parents listen to music when you were a teenager?

_____

What did your parents feel or have to say about your music preferences?

_____

_____

_____

Name _____ Date _____

Interview: Sing Out!

Person Interviewed: _____ Position: <u>Singer</u>

Do you sing mostly in a group or alone? _____

Where do you most often sing? _____

How long have you been doing this? _____

Is training required to do this? _____

What special training (if any) did you receive for this? _____

_____

Approximately how much time does this take per week? _____

Practicing vs. performing? _____

Do people get paid for this in some areas? _____

Here? _____

Do people do this full-time? _____ part-time? _____ volunteer? _____

Where do you get the music you use? _____

Who chooses the music you use? _____

Who pays for it? _____ About how much per year? _____

Who are some composers of the music you use? _____

_____

_____

Do you sing classical? _____ folk? _____ pop? _____ rock? _____ jazz? _____

Do you sing unaccompanied (a cappella)? _____

Are you accompanied by keyboard? ___ instrumental? (what) _____

What do you listen to for your own pleasure and/or relaxation? _____

_____

_____

_____

How would it change your life if you had to stop singing? _____

_____

_____

_____

If you could change one thing about your involvement in music, what would it be? _____

_____

_____

Interview: Play It Again, Sam

Person Interviewed: _____ Position: <u>Instrumentalist</u>

Do you play mostly in a group or alone? _____

Where do you most often play? _____

How long have you been doing this? _____

Is training required to do this? _____

What special training (if any) did you receive for this? _____

Do you play any other instruments? (name) _____

_____

Approximately how much time does this take per week? _____

Practicing vs. performing? _____

Do people get paid for this in some areas? _____ Here? _____

Do people do this full-time? _____ part-time? _____ volunteer? _____

Where do you get the music you use? _____

_____

Who chooses the music you use? _____

Who pays for it? _____ About how much per year? _____

Who are some composers of the music you use? _____

_____

_____

Do you play classical? _____ folk? _____ pop? _____ rock? _____ jazz? _____

In what other groups have you played? _____

_____

What do you listen to for your own pleasure and/or relaxation? _____

_____

_____

How would it change your life if you had to stop playing? _____

_____

_____

If you could change one thing about your involvement in music, what would it be? _____

_____

_____

Interview: Library Music

Person Interviewed: _____   Position: <u>Librarian</u>

Do you budget a specific amount for music resource purchases each year?

_____

Approximately how much do you generally spend on music resources each year? _____

How do you decide which music resource books to purchase?

_____

_____

_____

What are the most expensive music resources to purchase?

_____

What are the least expensive music resources to purchase?

_____

What music resources are used the most often?

_____

What music resources are used the least often?

_____

What music books are signed out the most often?

_____

What music books are signed out the least often?

_____

What music resource/book do you think students would like the most if they just gave it a chance? _____

_____

_____

What is the music resource you would most like to have that you don't have?

_____

_____

_____

Name _____ Date _____

Interview: Radio Disc Jockey

Person Interviewed: _____ Position: <u>Disc Jockey</u>

How does the music get chosen for each show? _____

_____

_____

_____

Approximately how many songs get played per hour? _____

How do the "Top 10" get chosen? _____

_____

How do you get your copies of the songs? _____

_____

What do you do with the old songs/tapes/records/CDs? _____

_____

What is the most popular song you remember? _____

_____

How long have you been doing this? _____

What kind of training prepared you for this job? _____

_____

_____

What is the part you like best? _____

_____

_____

_____

What is the part you like least? _____

_____

_____

_____

What is the biggest change you've seen? _____

_____

_____

What connection to music did you have when you were younger? _____

_____

_____

Name _____   Date _____

Interview: Music in Religion

Person Interviewed: _____ Position: _____
Religious Group: _____

How long have you been doing this? _____
Is training required to do this? _____
What special training (if any) did you receive for this? _____
_____
_____

Approximately how much time does this take per week? _____
Doing what? _____
Do people get paid for this in some areas? _____ Here? _____
Do people do this full-time? _____ part-time? _____ volunteer? _____
Describe the importance of music in your religious setting. _____
_____
_____
_____
_____

Where do you get the music you use? _____
_____

Who chooses the music you use? _____
_____

Who pays for it? _____
About how much per year? _____
Who are some composers of the music you use? _____
_____
_____

Does your religious setting use classical music? _____ folk music? _____
contemporary music? _____ pop style music? _____ vocal? _____
keyboard? _____ other instrumental? (what) _____
In what situations does music create a controversy in your religious setting?
_____
_____
_____

Name _____ Date _____

Interview: Tape Store Manager

Person Interviewed: _____ Position: <u>Manager</u>

Approximately how many records do you order each month? _____

Approximately how many tapes do you order each month?

single play _____ albums _____

Approximately how many CDs do you order each month? _____

How do you decide which ones and how many of each to buy? _____

_____

_____

_____

What is the most expensive type to purchase? _____

What is the least expensive type to purchase? _____

What type of music sells the most? _____

What type of music sells the least? _____

How long have you been doing this? _____

What is the part you like best? _____

_____

_____

_____

What is the part you like least? _____

_____

_____

_____

What is the biggest change you've seen? _____

_____

_____

_____

What connection to music did you have when you were younger? _____

_____

_____

_____

More Interview Ideas

There are many other careers involving music, which may or may not be represented in your area. Below is a far-from-complete list. Between it and the assignment variation ideas on p. 16, you should be able to get more than enough ideas. Consider doing the interview by mail or phone. Check the yellow pages and association directories in the library.

- Person responsible for selling air time on a radio station
- Person involved in manufacturing records
- Person working at a small or large recording studio
- Private instrumental instructor
- Private vocal teacher
- Person who sells background music
- Choir or chorus director
- Music director for local community theater
- Music director for high school musical
- Choreographer for high school musical
- Dance teacher
- Choreographer
- Figure skater
- Sound engineer for live concert
- Person who chooses music for local TV station
- Person who chooses music for local advertising agency
- Businessperson who uses music at the office
- Band or orchestra conductor
- Member of an amateur or professional rock group
- Surgeon who uses music in the operating room
- Therapist who uses music (music therapist, massage therapist)
- Pain control specialist who teaches use of music
- Jukebox distributor
- Restaurant owner/manager who uses taped music or music boxes
- Sound equipment store owner/manager/salesperson
- Sheet music store owner/manager/salesperson
- K–12 or college music instructor
- Booking agent for local civic center or auditorium

Remember to open your mind to careers that are not considered music careers but that use or connect to music in some way.

CONCEPT ATTAINMENT

WHAT?

Concept attainment is a model of teaching with clearly defined steps, easily used within a general music classroom. It does not require long teaching periods and is adaptable to a wide variety of music topics. The basic method involves a game in which students consider pairs of examples, one of which does fit a hidden concept and one of which does not. While comparing and contrasting these sets of examples, the students try to discover what the concept could be. Students test their theory, coming up with pairs of their own examples, then define the concept, and in conclusion discuss the thinking processes that they used.

WHEN?

Concept attainment works wonderfully at either end of a unit. As an introduction, it lets you assess the level of the class without boring those with a high level of understanding while encouraging and leading those with weaker skills. A great end-of-unit recap and review, it will meet with a more enthusiastic reception than a review sheet to take home and study. (*Note:* In my teaching, I consider the third stage of the model, analyzing thinking, especially important if using the lesson to begin a unit, less important if using it as a review.)

WHY?

We all know how much fun puzzles are. Kids think so, too. They are caught thinking (despite themselves!) with this model. Those who never raise their hands can be observed puzzling through and trying to guess the answer, intrigued. When I observe a concept attainment lesson, I find myself actively involved, comparing and contrasting, hypothesizing and analyzing, just as eager as the students to figure out what the teacher is thinking. The real blessings are that this model is involving, develops higher level thinking skills, teaches concepts, facilitates observational evaluation, and it is still fun!

HOW?

Read through the sample lesson plan that follows, and until you are comfortable with the model, keep the At a Glance chart handy. Start by using any of the sample lists that fit your curriculum and then go from there.

At a Glance

First Stage
Explain format
Set up and start list

Fast Version	**Longer Version**
Silently hypothesize	Students list/state hypotheses
Students test theories with new examples <u>or</u>	Add to example list and use to refute
Attempt to define concept	some hypotheses and explain why
	Continue until hypothesis confirmed

Second Stage
Students add examples
Restate definition

Third Stage
Analyze thinking process

Program Music

There are two versions of this game provided here: a fast version for more advanced students and a longer version for beginners.

LONGER VERSION

1. Explain the format: Tell students that you will be thinking of a musical idea or concept, and that they are to guess what the concept is. For clues, you will put examples on the board in two columns: a YES column containing examples that illustrate the concept, and a NO column containing examples that don't. After students examine the examples, they should try to identify the concept. You will list their hypotheses on the board. Then you will add more examples to the YES and NO columns. After each example, students will reexamine the list of hypotheses and eliminate the ones that no longer fit the examples. This will continue until all the wrong hypotheses have been eliminated and the right one is left.

2. Start by putting up a pair of examples on the board. For example, if the concept were "Program Music," your board would look like this:

Concept: _____

YES	NO
Nutcracker Suite/Tchaikovsky	Water Music/Handel

---

3. Solicit hypotheses from students and list them on the board. For the preceding example, you might get a list like this:

Music by Tchaikovsky	Christmas music	Holiday music
Children's stories in music	Russian composers	Fantasies

4. Add another pair of examples, and have students try to eliminate some hypotheses with this new information. For example, you could add *Peter and the Wolf* (Prokofiev) to YES and *Liebestraum* (Liszt) to NO. Let them tell you that this would eliminate Christmas music and holiday music. Be sure they explain *why*. Cross out or erase eliminated hypotheses.

5. Add another pair of examples, for instance *Carnival of the Animals* (Saint-Saëns) to YES and *Unfinished Symphony* (Schubert) to NO to eliminate Russian composers. Continue until students have eliminated all but the correct concept. Confirm by retracing how the others were eliminated.

FAST VERSION

1. Explain the format: Tell students you will be thinking of a musical idea or concept and that they are to guess what the concept is. For clues, you will put examples on the board in two columns: a YES column containing examples that illustrate the concept, and a NO column containing examples that don't. They should try to identify the concept, but not say it out loud. Instead, when they think they have the answer, they will give you a pair of examples for the YES and NO columns. If the examples do not fit your concept, someone else will try. If they do, the student will be asked to name the concept. Occasionally, a student will give a pair of examples that work, but will get the concept wrong. In that case, another student will try a pair of examples. This will continue until the concept is identified.

2. Start by putting up a pair of examples on the board. For example, if the concept were "Program Music," your board would look like this:

Concept: _____	
YES	NO
Nutcracker Suite/Tchaikovsky	Water Music/Handel

3. Remind students to hypothesize silently. When a student has a guess, ask for a pair of examples that would fit the concept. For example, if a student who thought the concept was Russian composers might suggest *Night on Bald Mountain* (Mussorgsky) for YES and *An American in Paris* (Gershwin) for NO. You would say the pair did not fit the concept, and ask another student to try, possibly adding another pair yourself, such as *Carnival of the Animals* (Saint-Saëns) to YES and *Unfinished Symphony* (Schubert) to NO.

4. If the pair of examples is correct, ask the student for the concept. For example, the student might give you *Peter and the Wolf* (Prokofiev) for YES and *Liebestraum* (Liszt) for NO, but then say the concept was Russian composers. You would say that the concept was wrong and ask for more pairs.

5. Continue until a student gives an appropriate pair of examples and correctly identifies the concept.

Once the concept is found, either by the fast or long version, you can go on to the second and third stages, outlined below. Sometimes the class will not get the concept and you will have to supply it. This does not mean the lesson has failed, nor have the students, nor you! It is the process that provides the learning, not the product.

SECOND STAGE

6. Students add examples: Involve more students by asking for more pairs to fit the concept. (*Hint:* It would give you more control over the specifics if you have a list of unlabeled examples from which students can draw the pairs. That way you control the repertoire that they will be offering.)

7. Restate the definition: Confirm correct examples and restate the definition of the concept, referring to the characteristics that you consider essential to the concept.

THIRD STAGE

8. Analyze the thinking process: Ask students to discuss their thoughts while trying to guess the concept. How you do this will vary with the age of class. (*Examples:* Describe what you did to form ideas/hypotheses. How did you try out ideas? How did you decide what characteristics the YESes had in common? How did you discover the ways the NOs contrasted? What strategies did you use? How many guesses did it take you?)

EXTENSIONS AND VARIATIONS

1. Do not limit yourself to written examples just because they may seem fastest. Try using aural, notated, or pictorial examples.

2. Let students prepare a concept attainment lesson.

3. Computer connection: Have students research and create a database of music, musicians, styles, etc., studied in class. Use for new puzzles.

A FINAL NOTE

It is tempting, in a time crunch, to stop after the first stage (successfully deducing the concept). Take the time to continue. Call on various students to continue providing examples. Testing their understanding of the concept by having them come up with their own examples lets you evaluate the understanding within the class. By having the class develop criteria for the concept, rather than listing them yourself, you can observe their level of thinking. Taking even just a few moments to discuss the thinking strategies used will boost their thinking skills and, after going through this model several times, you will find that your classes move much faster. The minutes you spend in the analyzing stage will save you time and teaching later.

Song Lists

SEASONAL MUSIC*

(Music designed to be appropriate for a particular occasion or season)

YES	NO
White Christmas	Home on the Range
Frosty the Snowman	Star-Spangled Banner
Jingle Bells	Twinkle, Twinkle
Easter Parade	Row, Row, Row Your Boat
Happy Birthday to You	We Are the World
School's Out for Summer	Chopsticks
See You in September	That's What Friends Are For

*(For nonseasonal music, reverse the columns.)

SACRED MUSIC*

(Music designed to express or reflect religious beliefs)

YES	NO
Away in a Manger	Home on the Range
The Messiah	The Nutcracker Suite
Jesu, Joy of Man's Desiring	White Christmas
Hanukkah, O Hanukkah	Jingle Bells
Kum Ba Yah	Deck the Halls
Swing Low, Sweet Chariot	Chopsticks

*(For secular music, reverse the columns.)

STORY OR LEGEND SONGS

(Music that tells a specific story or legend)

YES	NO
John Henry	I've Been Working on the Railroad
Casey Jones	Drill, Ye Tarriers, Drill
Molly Malone	Greensleeves
Jack Was Every Inch a Sailor	Drunken Sailor
Davy Crockett	Home on the Range
Clementine	Sixteen Tons

OCCUPATIONAL SONGS

(Music that describes or comes from a particular occupation)

YES	NO
Drill, Ye Tarriers, Drill	Marine's Hymn
I've Been Working on the Railroad	Wabash Cannonball
Erie Canal	Buffalo Gals
Day-O (The Banana Boat Song)	Sittin' on the Dock of the Bay
Blow, Ye Winds	My Bonnie Lies over the Ocean
John Henry	Johnny B. Goode
Molly Malone	Aura Lee
Pick a Bale of Cotton	Swing Low, Sweet Chariot

SILLY SONGS

(Music designed to be humorous or nonsensical)

YES	NO
Supercalifragilisticexpialidocious	Marine's Hymn
Found a Peanut	Jingle Bells
On Top of Spaghetti	On Top of Old Smokey
Rattlin' Bog	This Land Is Your Land
Drunken Sailor	Molly Malone
I Know an Old Woman Who Swallowed a Fly	Climb Every Mountain

SOCIAL ISSUE SONGS

(Music designed to take a stand on a social or political issue)

YES	NO
We Shall Overcome	Home on the Range
Blowin' in the Wind	Twinkle, Twinkle
This Land Is Your Land	Star-Spangled Banner
Do They Know It's Christmas?	Frère Jacques
That's What Friends Are For	Row, Row, Row Your Boat
We Are the World	Batman Theme
We Didn't Start the Fire	Don't Worry, Be Happy
Brother, Can You Spare a Dime?	Jingle Bells
I Am Woman	I Enjoy Being a Girl

HISTORICAL BALLADS

(Music that describes an actual event, with or without exaggeration)

YES	NO
Wreck of the Edmund Fitzgerald	I Know an Old Woman
Battle of New Orleans	Rattlin' Bog
Abraham, Martin, and John	Blowin' in the Wind
P.T. 109	Yesterday
The Great Ship (The Titanic)	Clementine

SONGS FROM OTHER COUNTRIES

YES	NO
London Bridge	Row, Row, Row Your Boat
Wreck of the Edmund Fitzgerald	Clementine
Molly Malone	Casey Jones
Funiculi, Funicula	B-I-N-G-O
Marching to Pretoria	She'll be Comin' Round the Mountain
Waltzing Matilda	Home on the Range
Frère Jacques	Sourwood Mountain

Instrument Lists

ETHNIC/FOLK INSTRUMENTS

YES	NO
guitar	cello
banjo	violin
harmonica	clarinet
steel drums	timpani
panpipes	flute
balalaika	string bass
kalimba	piano
sitar	trumpet

INSTRUMENTS THAT CAN COMBINE PITCHES

YES	NO
sitar	saxophone
kalimba	trombone
balalaika	bass drum
violin	trumpet
piano	oboe
harmonica	flute
xylophone	castanets

Tone Color Lists

RASPY, SCRATCHY, UNEVEN SOUNDS

YES	NO
tires on gravel	superhighway drive
buzzer	bell
nails/blackboard	tapping foot
rattlesnake	hummingbird
clarinet	flute
saxophone	triangle
ratchet	wood block
oboe	snare drum

CONTROLLABLE, CHANGEABLE PITCH

YES	NO
human voice	cat's meow
dinner chimes	raindrops
clarinet	maracas
flute	wood block
timpani	tambourine
saxophone	triangle
oboe	snare drum

Option: Try these using the actual instruments or taped sounds.

More Category Ideas

MELODY PATTERNS

On a melody instrument, play songs or melody fragments to teach any of the following concepts:

playing style: staccato/legato/combination
dynamics: piano/forte/crescendo/decrescendo
tempo: largo/moderato/presto/accelerando/ritardando
pitch: mostly steps/mostly skips/mostly repetition
meter: duple/triple/compound

MUSICAL FORMS AND STYLES

Use recordings or taped fragments to introduce/review the concepts of:

vocal/instrumental/combined
march/waltz/canon or fugue/concerto/symphony
ballad/blues/jazz/up tempo/folk
different eras: Baroque/Classical/Romantic/etc.
different composers: Gershwin/Bach/Sousa/Chopin/etc.
form: ABA/rondo/ABAB/etc.

VOCAL STYLES

Use recordings or taped fragments to introduce/review the concepts of:

solo/duet/ trio/quartet/chorus
all male/all female/mixed voices
unison/harmony/a cappella/accompanied
ballad/scat/folk/rap/rock
recitative/chant

INSTRUMENTAL COMBINATIONS

Use recordings or taped fragments to introduce/review concepts of:

electronic/acoustic
solo/duet/trio/quartet
chamber group/orchestra/combo
strings/woodwinds/brass/percussion/keyboard

UP AND MOVING

Teacher Guidelines

Sometimes it is nice to get a class up and moving for an activity. The following examples work especially well to review a lesson or unit. Each takes no more than a half hour of initial preparation and can be used for a portion of a class or an entire period. Once the class has tried each of these, they can be done with different content much more easily the next time.

Wonderful times to use these are on those frustrating days like "picture day," or when the teacher forgets to tell you that nine students will be on a field trip, or when half the class is missing with the flu. Even tough days like the ones before vacations are good opportunities for this kind of lesson. I often used them as a "carrot," allowing a class to earn a "game day." Did I tell them how much learning was involved, or that they would need higher-level thinking skills to do the games? Not until after they were into the games, having fun, and begging for more!

If you are feeling particularly generous, share these with your colleagues. Many of them work equally well in other subject areas. (One possible exception is "Can You Hum a Few Bars?")

Does your school system support interdisciplinary projects? Team up with another content area teacher. Work together to create a more global review. For example, work with an American history teacher to do "Who/What Am I?" mixing politicians, musicians, events, instruments, songs, etc., from the American Revolutionary War era. Try "And Venn Again . . . !" with the guidance department when the counselor is doing a career lesson. Include some musical careers and a discussion of the benefits of balancing career and recreational interests for a successful, joyful adult life.

Hint: Save the cards and other equipment you make for each game so that you can reuse them with other students, other lessons, or mixed together for general review.

Who Am I?

Try this old favorite with a musical twist. An interactive variation of "Twenty Questions," it involves everyone and avoids the "last man out" embarrassment.

PREPARATION

Make a list of content that you have studied. Put each item on an index card or piece of oaktag. Make one card for each student in your class.

IN CLASS

When class begins, tape a card to each student's back. Give the class time to wander around trying to discover their identities by asking yes or no questions to narrow the possibilities. After all but a few students have guessed their own identities, change the situation so that those who are stuck do not become too frustrated or discouraged. Have those students stand in front while the rest of the students go back to their seats. Then have each student turn around to show the class who they are. The rest of the class then should give clues until each identity is deduced.

Ideas for Narrowing Questions

Am I a person?

Did I perform *and* compose?
Was I successful before I died?
Was I a child prodigy? Did I write for orchestras?

Am I a composition?

Am I for orchestra? for keyboard? Do I have words?

MORE CONTENT POSSIBILITIES

specific composers   specific performers
specific compositions   time periods in music
musical styles (e.g., rock, ballad, folk, aria, concerto, rap, jazz)

And Venn Again . . . !

Most middle school students have been introduced in math classes to Venn diagrams for comparing and contrasting numbers. Venn diagrams use overlapping circles to illustrate similar and different features (see example below). Using that principle to make "human Venn diagrams" can be a lot of fun and can demonstrate the complexity of music and musicians.

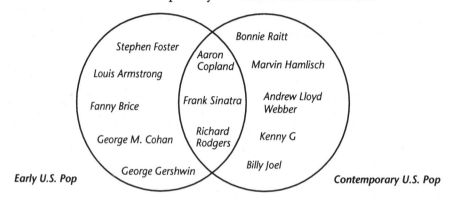

Early U.S. Pop   **Contemporary U.S. Pop**

PREPARATION

Make a card set for each category you plan to review. Use name cards from "Who Am I?" or add new cards to have enough for each class member.

IN CLASS

Pass out the identity cards and explain that these cards can be grouped in a variety of ways depending on what characteristics you choose to examine. Give an example. (For instance, George Gershwin could go in a category of symphonic music, Broadway, pop, vocal, instrumental, etc.) As you call off the characteristics, they are to sort themselves as quickly as possible by those characteristics, standing together in their groups. Call off different groupings. Do the checking as quickly as possible so that several groupings can be tried within the lesson. You don't need to wait until all the students have found a group. When most have found their group, have the class help those who are left.

VARIATION

If possible, make two or three large overlapping circles on the floor in chalk or masking tape. Use these like Venn diagram circles for the human groupings. If the class is not familiar with Venn diagrams, give a brief explanation and example on the board or do an interdisciplinary lesson with the math teacher. If you can't make the circles on the floor, have the people form the two circles, standing and facing in. The people who belong to both categories stand where the two circles intersect. (See the following example.)

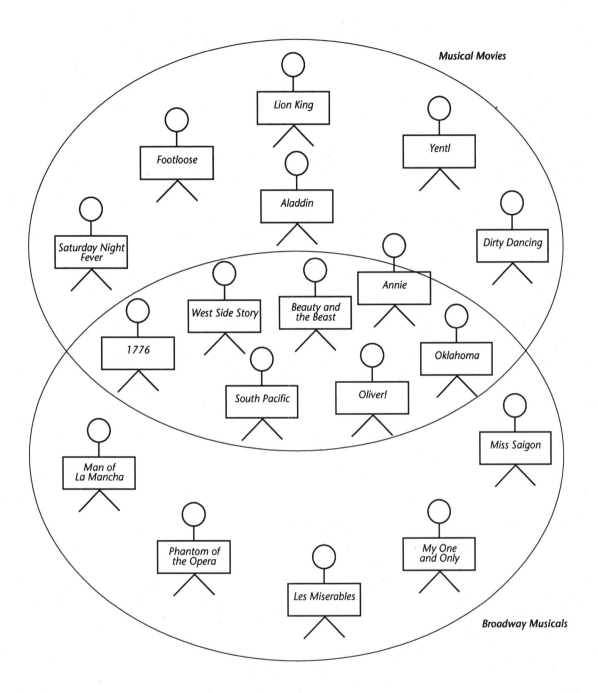

MORE CONTENT POSSIBILITIES

Singers/Instrumentalists   American/Foreign

Popular/Classical   Composers/Performers

When success came (in childhood/adulthood/after death)

Duple meter, triple, compound (use written out measures)

Can You Hum a Few Bars?

If you have a day when you and those around you can handle a little noise, this review game can be a lot of fun and a lot of learning.

PREPARATION

Make two sets of cards. On one set, write the names of the musical compositions that you are reviewing. On the other set, write the composers of each. (Decide whether you want only one possible match for each composer or whether you are willing to have groupings with one composer and several compositions.) You will need enough so that each student can have a card.

IN CLASS

Explain that you are passing out secret identity cards to each person in class. Some will receive the name of a composer, and some will receive the name of a musical composition. Those who are composers must wander around the class listening for a melody which they wrote. Those with titles must wander around humming the melody on their card until they find their composer. When composer and composition find one another, they should stand together and stop humming. When the room is silent (finally), review the results with the class.

SAMPLE PAIRINGS: COMPOSERS AND THEIR COMPOSITIONS

Mildred and Patty Hill	"Happy Birthday"
Franz Schubert	"Unfinished Symphony" theme
George F. Handel	"Hallelujah" Chorus
Irving Berlin	"God Bless America"
Stephen Foster	"Old Folks At Home"
George M. Cohan	"Yankee Doodle Dandy"

OTHERS TO TRY

folk songs and their countries   songs and their style

Paper Ball Catch

Playing catch with a class of adolescents can definitely be dangerous to you and your students' health, not to mention the windows, lights, and your sanity! With this activity you can have all the fun of playing catch, minus the hassles, accident reports, and visits to the nurse. You can also hold a full class review without putting anxious students on the spot and yet encouraging full participation at each child's level. Best of all . . . it's fast and fun!

PREPARATION

Make a paper ball by scrunching up a piece of paper, then adding another layer, and another, and another until the ball of loosely scrunched paper is about the size of a cantaloupe. Wrap masking tape around it to hold it together. Make a second ball using paper of a different color. Pick a category or topic that connects to your current curriculum content and that can be described/detailed in a list of information. Arrange the class in a circle, or have them turn their chairs/desks facing the center so that everyone can see everyone else in class. Decide whether you or the students will think up and ask the questions.

IN CLASS

Explain that you are going to conduct a group review of what the class has learned about _____. Tell students that the review is a game of catch. A review question will be asked; students with the answer should raise their hand, and the ball will be thrown to one of them. When they get the ball, they can call out their answer. The student with the ball then throws it to someone else. First rule: You don't throw the ball to students who don't have their hand up. Second rule: You try to throw it to someone who hasn't answered yet. Third rule: If you think someone has given an incorrect answer, you say "Stop" and give your reasons. The object is to see how long and how quickly the class can keep the ball going. (You can restart if it bogs down.)

VARIATION 1

For a real challenge, add the second ball. Until students get used to it, let both balls mean the same thing. Later, if the class is doing really well, vary it. For example, if the topic is a specific composer, receiving the white ball might mean giving a fact about the composer's life and the green ball might mean giving the title of something the composer wrote. It can get really crazy, but it is a ton of fun and does wonders for motivating quick and varied recall. Don't try this until they are really good with one ball.

VARIATION 2

Instead of using information lists, ask for information pairs on the general topic and use only one ball. This time, the person who answers correctly gives the next prompt. For example, if American composers and their music is the general topic and the previous one was George Gershwin, you might answer "Rhapsody in Blue" if you got the ball. You could then call another composer (e.g., Stephen Foster) or composition ("Swanee River") and toss the ball to one of students with their hand up.)

MORE CONTENT POSSIBILITIES

Information pairs

- composers and their compositions
- folk songs and their countries
- songs and their style

Lists of information

- Broadway composers
- symphonic instruments
- a specific composer or performer

- seasonal songs
- songs and their decades
- songs from movies
- Broadway shows

And Then What Happened?

Try this physical twist to involve a whole group in thinking through the sequence of musical events.

PREPARATION

Make a list of 12 to 15 musical events, and put each event on an index card. Make another set using a different color pen or marker, but otherwise identical. Be sure that the class has studied time lines and understands how to read and use a time line. (Try checking with the social studies or science teacher to be sure.)

IN CLASS

Pass out one card to each student. Challenge the students to arrange themselves in the proper sequence with other cards of their color. Explain that there will be two time lines when they are through. Set a time limit if you wish. After the two lines are formed, have students face each other and compare the time lines. Discuss any differences and correct any mistakes. Discuss how they worked through the problem, and come up with some strategies students can use to associate time frames and facts.

STARTER VERSION

- Start small. Give out four or five cards and see if those few students can arrange themselves in the proper order in front of the class. When the line is complete, the observers challenge anyone they think is misplaced, correcting the placement and explaining their reasoning. (Example below.)

VARIATIONS

- Try it with half the class making the time line and half watching. Observers correct and explain, as in the starter version.
- Focus on general time groupings rather than exact sequence. Make a time line in chalk or masking tape on the floor and use oaktag labels to mark the year divisions (see diagrammed example). Have students physically stand in the correct time period. Students demonstrate an overall sense of what happened when, without needing to have a precise year or exact sequence. This is less precise but is closer to the way we generally use sequence knowledge in real life.

MORE CONTENT POSSIBILITIES

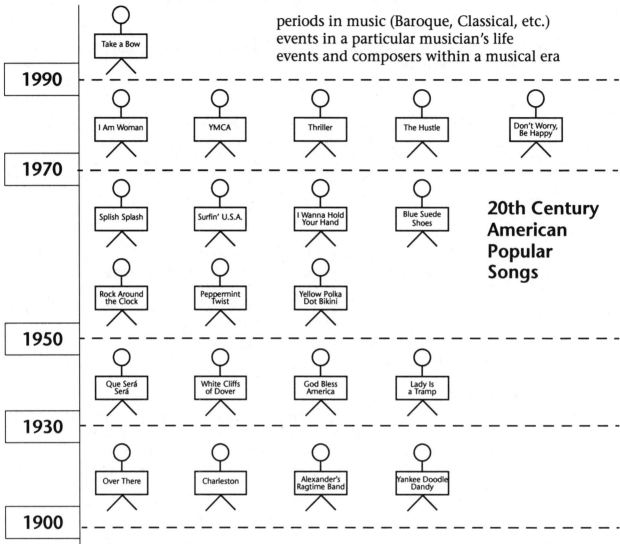

periods in music (Baroque, Classical, etc.)
events in a particular musician's life
events and composers within a musical era

20th Century American Popular Songs

Who's on the Line?

Try this to involve a whole group in deductive thinking and creativity.

PREPARATION

Get a phone from a yard sale or phone store. It does not need to work; in fact I use just the hand part with a dangling cord.

IN CLASS

Have a student "get a phone call" from a composer, performer, or person studied. The student uses the phone call to give clues about who the caller is while the rest of the class tries to guess the caller's identity.

KIDS DON'T GET IT?

Get a copy of an old recording of one of Bob Newhart's phone routines and let them hear one or two to get the idea. Or, do them yourself to let them see different ways it can be done. The students will want to get in on the act very soon.

VARIATIONS

- Let students do composer reports in this form as a means of teaching new information rather than review.
- Set a time limit and, at the end, students write down who they thought the caller was. (Everyone in class gives an answer, rather than just the first one to get it.)
- Set rules increasing the difficulty. (For example, you can't name specific compositions, just describe them.)
- Have the phone call be about a composer. Two people can do this version and plant clues for the class in their conversation. (An easy one follows.)

Instrumental Charades

Try this physical twist to involve a whole group in thinking through the different musical instruments, their categories, and the ways they are played.

PREPARATION

Make a set of instrument name cards. To make the set more flexible, try using different color pens or markers for different categories of instruments (classical, folk, ethnic, etc.).

IN CLASS

Explain that a volunteer will draw a card from the pile and pantomime for the rest of the class how that instrument is played. Challenge the observing students to identify the instrument by observing carefully. (See hints.) Explain which instrument category will be used. Set a time limit if you wish to keep the game moving and to keep everyone involved. When students correctly identify the instrument, ask how they worked it out. This will help others plan their pantomime and figure out other pantomimes. The first student to guess correctly chooses the next card. Play continues as time or interest suggests.

VARIATIONS

- Have the students prepare their instrument for playing before beginning to play (for instance, screwing on a clarinet reed, tuning a timpani, assembling a flute).
- Divide the class into teams. Have students watch the entire pantomime in silence and then write their guess on individual pieces of paper. Each team gets one point for each team member who had the correct answer. For the pantomimer, choose volunteers from alternating teams.
- Mix several instrument categories together.

HINTS

Consider such things as size, hand placement, hand/finger/foot use.

For example:

flute: hands spaced to side at mouth level, spaced apart, right hand curved front, left hand curved back, mouth pursed

piccolo: mouth pursed, hands the same as flute except side-by-side right next to mouth

clarinet: hands vertically in front, left above, right below, mouth's lower lip "rolled" under upper lip

saxophone: mouth the same as clarinet but head is usually tilted, hand placement is to the right side, with right elbow almost in line with right shoulder

organ: sitting, both feet moving along imaginary footboard, hands at different levels to indicate manuals, occasionally reach up and push down an organ stop, occasionally on the same manual

MORE CONTENT POSSIBILITIES

- symphonic, keyboard, ancient instruments
- American folk instruments (e.g., harmonica, banjo, mouth harp, spoons, guitar, "gutbucket")
- ethnic folk instruments (e.g., maracas, sitar, guiro, alphorn, steel drums, kalimba, pan flute)

INDUCTIVE LEARNING

WHAT?

Inductive learning is a model of teaching in which students discover and develop an understanding rather than receiving information from teacher demonstrations or lectures. Inductive learning lends itself especially well to classrooms familiar with cooperative learning groups and techniques. Students develop a concept by examining a group of ideas, facts, or objects; observing similarities and differences; grouping them accordingly; and using all of that to develop rules that they can use.

WHEN?

Inductive lessons give you a wonderful chance to observe the way your students think. If done as a full class lesson, you can observe and listen as you moderate the discussions. If done in cooperative groups, you have an even better chance to observe the musical thinking of class members. Inductive lessons are not exactly sit-in-your seats-still-as-mice lessons, so choose the timing carefully. Because discussions (or sound explorations) can get both lively and noisy, these lessons are not recommended for the day before vacation or any other time when student energy is especially high.

WHY?

As in concept attainment lessons, inductive lessons entice students to think (despite themselves!). Once they make the first step, even reluctant students are drawn into the puzzle, grouping and regrouping examples, trying and testing rules. This model also develops higher-level thinking skills and encourages diversity in thought.

HOW?

Letting the class discover things themselves can be more difficult to plan and take longer than simply telling them. Used to introduce a unit, inductive learning may seem at first to take far too long. You may think it is quicker to instruct. But by allowing students to develop the concept and rules, the understanding is so much solider that you will usually find the rest of the unit going much faster, much better, and the lost time will be made up before you know it. Try any of these three different sample lessons to decide which style works best for you. Then experiment on your own.

At a Glance

First Stage
Explain format
Post or distribute examples

Second Stage
Students discuss examples
Students explore possibilities and select a grouping

Third Stage
Students group the examples
Students develop a rule for groupings

Fourth Stage
Check the rule against given examples
Test the rule with new examples

Magnetic Learning Centers

If you have a little money and time to prepare, try making a large magnetic display set that you can use for grouping lessons. Put small magnets on the back of each card, using self-stick magnetic tape or hot glue. This makes exploring the groupings much easier since you will be able to move the cards as students suggest groupings. For the display board, try purchasing a metal countertop protector. You can cover the design with plain contact paper or very large cookie sheet(s) countertop protector. Before you buy either, be sure it is magnetic. For less than $10 you will have a learning center that is useful in many teaching situations.

Instrument Families

Objectives: To teach instrument families.
                To show how sound producers and starters affect tone color/ lead to family development.

Materials: Instrument card set (make cards for variety of familiar common and ethnic instruments, perhaps with names on one side, pictures on the other), blank cards/paper, magic markers, tape

First Stage

1. Explain format: Ask the class (can be new or review)—
   What do we mean by sound *producer*? examples?
   (What actually makes the sound—string, column of air, etc.)
   What do we mean by sound *starter*? examples?
   (What makes the sound start—plucking, blowing, beating, etc.)

   "Today I'm going to let you develop a way of grouping instruments and rules that will help others understand those groupings. We could do this in small cooperative groups, but since this is a new kind of lesson, we'll do it all together as a class today."

2. Post examples: Ask class to name as many instruments as they can. (Call on one student at a time.) Post each instrument on the board as it is named, using prewritten cards from card set or making new ones. Describe any unusual or unfamiliar ones.

Second Stage

3. Discuss examples: Brainstorm ways to group the instruments posted— by starter, by producer, by family, etc. Continue to generate different possible ways of grouping the instruments until you have a variety for the students to explore. You may wish to jot down the possibilities on the board.

4. Explore and select: Discuss several of the groupings and explore them by putting checks, stars, or other marks next to instruments that belong to a common group. Discuss problems as they arise. Eventually the class will settle on a grouping system that looks as if it will work for all of the examples. (For the purpose of this sample lesson, we will assume they choose the traditional instrument families. You may lead them to it, but try to give them time to get there themselves.)

Third Stage

5. Group examples: Have students name each group and make a column for each (premade cards, or make new ones). Post these papers on a wall or someplace convenient and visible. Ask students to get one or

two cards each and tape them on the paper where they feel each belongs.

RULES: 1. If a student is stuck, he or she may not ask which family.

2. A student may ask someone to describe the instrument or how it is played.

6. Develop a rule: When all instrument cards are placed into the groupings, discuss what makes a brass a brass, a percussion a percussion, etc. Encourage the class to create a rule for each family grouping. As each rule is generated, write it on a card and post it next to the family name.

Fourth Stage

7. Check the rule: Ask the class to look over the posted lists and see if they spot any instruments that should be moved to another category now that they have the rules. Challenge by asking why.

8. Test the rule: After all the groupings are checked, ask whether anyone can think of another instrument for any of the categories. If they name an instrument and a category, again check their thinking by asking why. If they can't, you describe an instrument and see if they can figure out which family it belongs to and explain why.

LESSON EXTENSIONS

1. Assign independent practice as homework, puzzle, or game.

2. Repeat steps 3 to 8, grouping the instruments a different way. Discuss how that changed the groupings.

3. Try instruments from other countries and cultures, having students see if their rules still work. Discuss common factors in the development of instruments from culture to culture.

4. Post instrument family learning center.

Time Signatures

Objectives: To introduce or review time signatures.
To review note/rest values.

Materials: Measure Cards set (see reproducible pp. 126–129) copied and cut, blank measure cards or paper slips for student use

Teaching Outline
(Mixed full class and small groups)

1. Introduction: Review note values ($\quad$ = 1 beat). Remind students that rests are the same as beats, but beats of silence—not beats of sound.

2. Post measure cards on board or bulletin board. As you're doing that, ask the class to be watching as they will be asked next how the cards could be grouped. Instruct them to be thinking which cards belong together and why. Be sure to mix the cards around as you post them.

3–4. Discussion and exploration: Have the class generate possibilities for grouping. Lead to grouping by total number of beats.

5. Group the cards by category (2, 3, 4): Check on the thinking process. (Ask: "Why does it fit that category?" repeatedly to reinforce the note and rest values. Say: "Show me how it fits.") Have the class check for errors, again reinforcing the thinking process until all cards are grouped correctly.

6. Develop a rule for the groupings: Through class discussion, develop a specific rule for grouping that the class feels will work.

7. Check the rule: Divide the class into pairs, threes, fours, whatever. Pass out blank cards or papers and ask each group to write out two additional examples for each category, using the rule the class generated. Then have each group or pair post their examples in the proper category. As a class, check the newly posted cards. If needed, briefly repeat steps 5 and 6, revising the rule until an acceptable rule has been generated and checked. Explain and demonstrate how time signatures developed to fill this need for groupings and a rule to explain groupings. Option: With older students, a discussion of natural accents can fit here.

8. Test the rule: Using time signatures, try a few more examples as a group. Assign independent practice on time-signature beat groupings.

Tone Color

Objectives: 1. To explore different tone colors.
2. To explore and show how many different ways musical sounds and instruments can be grouped.

Materials: Instrument/tone color boxes (one per group)—these are just boxes you fill with folk and rhythm instruments and other objects that can produce a wide variety of tone colors. (example: finger cymbals, maracas, triangle, kazoo, mouth harp, harmonica, spoons, etc.), project outline and worksheet (pp. 53, 54)

Teaching Outline

1. Introduction: Break the class into learning groups. Review previous class discussions of tone color—what it is, how it is made, etc. Pass a project outline and worksheet to each group. Answer questions. Review class rules for working in groups.

2. Post examples: Pass out one tone color/instrument box and exploration worksheet to each group.

3–4. Discussion and exploration: Generate different possible ways of grouping the instruments in the box. Encourage sound experimentation.

5. Group the examples: Have each group write down their chosen headings on the worksheet and then list the instruments in that grouping.

6. Develop a rule for groupings: Have each group discuss how they choose a group for each instrument. Each small group should create a rule for each grouping and write it on the worksheet.

7–8. Check and test the rule:

   a. Ask each group to look over their lists and see if they spot any instruments that should be moved to another category now that they've written the rules.

   b. Have each group generate at least two more examples of sounds for each of their categories. If you like, allow them to include non-traditional musical sounds, e.g., nature sounds or mechanical sounds. Remind them to check their thinking by asking why they put each sound in that category.

Follow-up: Have groups report back to the whole class. Discuss different ways of grouping, problems, etc. Discuss implications and possible conclusions.

Name _____ Date _____

Tone Color Exploration/Outline

Objectives: To explore different tone colors.
To explore some of the many ways musical sounds and instruments can be grouped.

Materials: Instrument/tone color "boxes" (one per group)
Project outlines and worksheets (one set per group)

Remember to follow the rules of working in groups!

PROJECT OUTLINE

Group discussion: Experiment with the different sounds that the instruments in your box can make. (Be careful with the instruments, of course.) Working in your group, discuss different possible ways of grouping the instruments in your box.

Group the cards: Experiment with different ways of grouping them. When your group agrees on a set of groupings, list the instruments in each group on your worksheet.

Develop a rule for groupings: Discuss how you chose which group for each instrument. Create a rule to describe each grouping. Write your rule on your worksheet.

Check the rule: Look over your lists and see if there are any instruments that should be moved to another category now that you have written the grouping rules. Working together, think of at least two more examples of sounds for each of your categories. Remember to check your thinking by asking why they go in that category.

FOLLOW-UP

Report back to the whole class. Be ready to explain:

- what groupings you choose
- how you went about the first grouping
- what was hardest/easiest

Listen to the reports from the other groups.
Discuss the differences and similarities.

Tone Color Exploration/Worksheet

First Group: _____

All sounds in this group _____
What else might go in this group?

Second Group: _____

All sounds in this group _____
What else might go in this group?

Third Group: _____

All sounds in this group _____
What else might go in this group?

Fourth Group: _____

All sounds in this group _____
What else might go in this group?

Leftovers?

More Inductive Learning Ideas

This chapter has provided you with three separate lessons using the inductive model of teaching. This method is excellent for developing and expanding higher-level thinking skills, problem solving strategies, and the art of working cooperatively in groups. It can be used with a wide variety of curriculum topics, both to introduce and to review concepts.

Inductive lessons can be done with any content that can be grouped or categorized according to rules or guidelines. They are often modified and combined with other lesson models. For example, in the simulation section you will find three repertoire lessons that are also a variation of the inductive model:

Song Assembly (pp. 58–61)

Symphony Board (pp. 65–67)

Interim Conductor (pp. 65, 68–69)

If you read through the repertoire ideas (see p. 93), you will see that with very little effort they can be done in a full or modified inductive style. You can also get ideas from the Concept Attainment chapter groupings, pp. 27–35.

MORE POSSIBILITIES

Play a variety of musical excerpts, or post cards with a wide variety of musical selections, and have students group and generate rules for their groupings.

- musical genre (Broadway, pop, classical, jazz, etc.)
- groupings (solo, duet, quartet, ensembles, orchestra, etc.)
- song form (ballad, chant, oratorio, opera, musical, etc.)
- timbre (different instrumental sounds)
- pitch range (high, low, middle, narrow or wide, etc.)
- tonality (major, minor, atonal, etc.)
- rhythmic style (march, waltz, ragtime, etc.)
- musical periods (Baroque, Classical, Romantic, etc.)

ROLE-PLAYS AND SIMULATIONS

Teacher Guidelines

1. Role-plays and simulations are time flexible.

   Role-play lessons can be used in those "There's five minutes left. What do I do?" situations. They can also be the center of a multilesson arc or even a school-wide theme project.

2. Role-plays and simulations are curriculum flexible.

   Role-play lessons can be used to introduce a unit and start students thinking or as the culminating lesson that pulls everything together.

3. Vary the type of role-play or simulation.

   Sometimes do a role-play with only two to four students in front of the full class. Other times involve the entire class.

4. Assign roles against stereotypes.

   Assign the sports hero to be the composer's mother and you will be sure every student in class will be watching to see what happens! Assign your heavy-metal fan to role-play in favor of record content ratings and really stretch his or her thinking!

5. Set students up for success.

   —If you are doing an "instant" role-play, be sure to give two to three minutes of hall time and a thought starter to each participant. (As an example, see the John Philip Sousa role-play on pp. 79–83.) Allow space for players to jot ideas.

   —If you are doing a role-play using material unfamiliar to the students, prepare them with some prediscussion, research hints, or starters.

6. Build on student involvement.

   Any observers of a role-play are thinking how they would have done it differently. Use that. Whenever possible, immediately repeat the role-play or a piece of it, recasting from the observers.

7. Mix, match, and modify.

   Use role-plays to spice and entice, not as the full curriculum. Adapt these to fit your curriculum, not the reverse. Let students propose and design role-play lessons using the preparation sheet on p. 125. Some will be great. Try them!

At a Glance

Before Lesson

Copy/prepare student materials.
Plan for any special room setup.
(Option: Arrange for videotape.)

During Lesson

Step One: Explain format

Set up situation.
Explore issues and topics to be addressed.

Step Two: Explain responsibilities

Discuss roles and assign students.
Discuss task of role-play observers.

Step Three: Do the role-play or simulation

Step Four: Evaluate results

Discuss what happened during the role-play.
Discuss issues, positions, etc.
Discuss possible changes.
Connect to personal issues or current trends.

Note: Steps 3 and 4 can be repeated if desired with revised roles or reassigned student players and observers.

After Lesson

Assign follow-up activity. This can be as simple as a discussion or, if individual response is needed, something written.

Song Assembly

BEFORE LESSON

Teacher Preparation

_____ Become familiar with the situation setup.

_____ Review repertoire list. Be sure all are familiar to your students.

(Option: Type in any other songs that are familiar to your students.)

_____ Check the list to be sure your students can find several possible themes (seasonal, rounds, pattern songs, patriotic, etc.). For sample list with categories, see p. 132–133.

_____ Make enough copies of the student info sheet for your class.

_____ Decide how you will break the class into teams and make seating rearrangements if you choose.

_____ Run off copies of worksheet for each team. If you prefer, make overheads of the blank worksheets and give each team a marker, or use large chart paper and markers instead. (*Note:* The Step Three section of the worksheet on p. 61 is an optional extension. It can be included for each team, done orally during debriefing discussions, or skipped.)

Class Preparation

_____ Discuss student experiences with assemblies when they were younger (length? selections? variety? style? etc.). This can be less than five minutes at the end of the class, before the lesson, or at the beginning of the lesson.

LESSON DAY

Do intro mini-discussion about singing assemblies.	5 min
Read aloud/review situation setup.	
Explain or review rules.	5 min
Break class into committees.	
Pass out info sheets and worksheets.	
If you are using overheads or chart paper and markers, pass them out, too.	
Monitor groups as they work, assisting if needed.	20 min

Debriefing Activity

Use a reporter from each committee or post chart paper programs or project programs on overhead projector.	15 min
Discuss choices and the variety of possibilities.	

Name _____ Date _____

Simulation: Song Assembly

SITUATION SETUP

You have been asked to plan an assembly for the elementary students in grades one to three. Below is a list of the songs the children already know. Your chorus also knows them. Your chorus knows some of the theme songs from recent hit movies and several TV shows.

When you perform assemblies, you always give a brief introduction to each section of three or four songs, explaining to the audience something about the songs and how they are connected. The assembly is limited to 40 minutes, since it will be held during your regular chorus period. Each song lasts about 3 minutes, but to leave time for introductions you must limit the program to 10 songs. The concert must include at least one round and one sing-along section. You must also include at least three songs the children may not know, but which you think they will enjoy. Since time is limited, you might decide to write out the introductions so you can be sure everything fits in the 40 minutes allowed and the students will not be late for their next class.

SONGS THE AUDIENCE KNOWS

Alouette

America (My Country 'Tis of Thee)

Clementine

I've Been Working on the Railroad

Row, Row, Row Your Boat

She'll Be Comin' Round the Mountain

Star-Spangled Banner

Twinkle, Twinkle Little Star

He's Got the Whole World in His Hands

Frere Jacques

B-I-N-G-O

Happy Birthday

A Ram Sam Sam

Waltzing Matilda

Kum Ba Yah

You're a Grand Old Flag

Yankee Doodle

Three Blind Mice

Simulation: Song Assembly/Worksheet

Step One: Write in the song titles you have chosen for the assembly. Remember your requirements and limits.

Sing-along song(s):

_____ (a round)

_____

_____

_____

Songs the audience knows:

_____

_____

_____

New songs the audience will enjoy:

_____

_____

_____

Step Two: Put the songs in order for the concert, grouped by themes. Write in a theme title for each group and skip a line between each group. Each section must contain at least two songs.

_____

_____

_____

_____

_____

_____

_____

(continued)

Simulation: Song Assembly/Worksheet *(continued)*

Step Three: Write in the theme titles for each song group and the brief intro-
duction/explanation for each section.

Title: _____

Introduction: _____

_____

_____

_____

Title: _____

Introduction: _____

_____

_____

_____

Title: _____

Introduction: _____

_____

_____

_____

Title: _____

Introduction: _____

_____

_____

_____

WKID Radio

BEFORE LESSON

Teacher Preparation

_____ Become familiar with the situation setup.

_____ Decide what limits you wish to impose regarding lyrics and style. (Option: You could limit the youth programs to a specific form or category of music to avoid this issue.)

_____ Decide whether lesson will be done as homework or class work.

_____ Make enough copies of the student info sheet for your class.

_____ Make enough copies of the application form for your class.

_____ Decide if you will break the class into teams or if you will allow free choice for applicant combinations.

_____ Decide whether students will just fill in the application, or extend the project by making an audiotape of their program.

Class Preparation

_____ Discuss the different radio formats (e.g., rock, classical, talk, easy listening, middle of the road, etc.).

_____ Discuss the patterns within a radio hour (ratio of music to talk? length? selections? variety? style?).

These discussions can take less than 10 minutes at the end of the class, before the lesson, at the beginning of the lesson, or can be expanded to full lessons in their own right.

LESSON DAY

Do intro mini-discussion about radio programming. Read aloud/review situation setup.	5 min
Explain or review rules.	5 min
Break class into small groups of applicants. Pass out info sheets and worksheets. You could choose to make overheads of blank applications and give each team a marker, or use large chart paper and markers. Monitor groups as they work, assisting if needed. (If lesson is done as homework, skip this.)	20 min

Debriefing Activity

(If lesson is homework, try this as a follow-up lesson.) Share applications. Read, duplicate, project on overhead, or post chart paper programs. Discuss choices and the variety of possibilities.	15 min

Simulation: WKID Radio

SITUATION SETUP

The local radio station, WKID, has just been sold. The new owners intend to air a wide variety of music styles rather than a single format. In an attempt to gain new listeners they are beginning a new policy. Each Saturday, all of the disc jockeys will be young people. There is an application process for students interested in hosting a program. Students may apply as individuals or in teams of two or three. Students can choose to host a program of one or two hours so that many will have the opportunity to participate.

Each program must have a theme so that listeners will be encouraged to stay tuned to the entire program. Each selection should connect to the chosen theme. Any theme that does not conflict with the station's standards is acceptable. (If in doubt about the content of lyrics, check with the station.) Any style of music is possible. Themes can be a period of time, a composer, a performer, a style, a history, or a topic.

Students should do their best, as the owners are considering hiring several students to host shows on a regular basis. Student applications will be judged on how creative they are, how accurate their information is, whether they have followed the guidelines, and what facts they have gathered to work into their on-air chatter.

HINTS AND REMINDERS

- Start by brainstorming a list of possible themes. Then narrow it down to a few that you can research easily. After checking out the information available, make your final theme choice.

- Be sure your selections stay within the time limit, and leave time between each selection for your on-air chatter about the theme and the music.

- Be sure that for each selection you have a fact about its background, history, or performer to share with and interest your radio listeners.

Name _____ Date _____

Simulation: WKID Radio/Application

NAME(S): _____

SCHOOL: _____ TEACHER: _____ GRADE: ___

APPLICATION DATE: _____ PROGRAM: (check one) ___1 hr ___2 hr

PROGRAM THEME: _____

Selection	Composer/Performer	Length
_____	_____	_____
_____	_____	_____
_____	_____	_____
_____	_____	_____
_____	_____	_____
_____	_____	_____
_____	_____	_____

Facts/background you plan to include on-air.

_____

_____

_____

_____

_____

_____

_____

_____

You may use the back of this application if necessary.

       Creative Activities for Music and Humanities Classes

Symphony Board and Interim Conductor

BEFORE LESSON

Teacher Preparation

_____ Become familiar with the situation setup.

_____ Prepare a repertoire list based on the music listening activities your students have had. (For sample list, see pp. 134–135.)

_____ Add any other musical selections with which all of your students are familiar.

_____ Check the list to be sure that there are several possible themes (composer? country? musical period? genre? titles?).

_____ Make enough copies of the list for your class.

_____ Decide how you will break the class into teams, and make seating rearrangements if you choose.

_____ Run off copies of worksheet for each team. If you prefer, make overheads of the blank worksheets and give each team a marker, or use large chart paper and markers instead.

Class Preparation

_____ Discuss previous student experiences or opinions of symphony concerts (length? selections? variety? style?). This can be less than five minutes at the end of the class, before the lesson, or at the beginning of the lesson.

LESSON DAY

Do intro mini-discussion about orchestra programs.   5 min
Explain or review setting/premise.
Explain or review rules.   5 min
Break class into committees.
Pass out lists and worksheets.
If you are using overheads or charts and markers, pass them out, too.
Monitor groups as they work, assisting if needed.   20 min

Debriefing Activity

Use a reporter from each committee, or post chart paper
programs or project programs on overhead projector.   15 min
Discuss choices and the variety of possibilities.

Simulation: Symphony Board

SITUATION SETUP

You are on the board of directors of a well-known and very successful city orchestra. Unfortunately, the conductor unexpectedly has been taken seriously ill. You and the rest of the board have hired a young, successful, and talented symphony orchestra conductor to fill out the year, but he cannot take over until one week before the first concert. He will plan the rest of the season, but asks that the board choose the program for the first concert. He has sent a list of the selections he is interested in conducting and the board has compared it with the orchestra's repertoire. You and your committee must select the concert program.

The attached list of musical compositions is what you must use to choose the program. Since the orchestra is talented, experienced, and learns new material quickly, you may add one or two selections which are not on the repertoire list for the concert. The concertmaster will rehearse the new music with the orchestra until the new conductor arrives. As usual, the concert will contain eight selections with an intermission halfway through. To help ticket sales, you must focus each concert around a common theme. Put that theme at the top of the concert list. If the theme title does not explain the common bond, add a note explaining the connection between selections.

GUIDELINES

- The concert must have eight selections.
- The selections must be connected by a theme.
- The concert should include one or two new selections.

OPTIONS

- A mixture of styles is strongly recommended.
- One half of the concert could include lighter or pop selections.
- You may include some vocal music. A chorus and soloists are available.

Name _____ Date _____

Simulation: Symphony Board/Worksheet

PROCEDURE

(Check off when each is done.)

_____ Step 1—Look over the repertoire list.

_____ Step 2—Brainstorm some things the selections have in common.

_____ Step 3—Choose a theme.

_____ Step 4—Choose five to seven selections that fit the theme.

_____ Step 5—Choose one to three new selections that fit the theme.

_____ Step 6—Put the selections in order for each half of the concert.

_____ Step 7—Write your final theme and concert program below.

Remember—Work together as a team!

Concert Theme:

_____

_____

_____

_____

Intermission

_____

_____

_____

_____

Simulation: Interim Conductor

SITUATION SETUP

You are a young, successful, and talented symphony orchestra conductor. You have just been hired for one year to replace the regular conductor of a well-known and very successful city orchestra. The board of directors has sent you the attached list of the musical compositions currently in the orchestra's repertoire. The orchestra can play any of these selections. You must now propose two concert programs, using the given repertoire, which will follow the opening concert designed by the symphony's board. Since the orchestra is talented, experienced, and learns new material quickly, the board feels you may add up to three selections that are not on the repertoire list for each concert. The board suggests that you include at least one new selection each concert. Each concert should contain approximately eight selections with an intermission about halfway through.

To help ticket sales, please focus each concert around a common theme and put that theme at the top of each concert list. If the theme title does not explain the common bond, please add a note explaining the connection between selections.

GUIDELINES

- Each concert must have eight selections.
- The selections must be connected by a theme.
- Each concert must include between one and three new selections.

OPTIONS

- A mixture of styles is strongly recommended.
- At least one concert should include lighter or pop selections.
- You may include some vocal music. A chorus and soloists are available.
- You should not repeat a selection during the season.

Simulation: Interim Conductor/Worksheet

GUIDELINES

- Use the repertoire list given.
- Each concert must have eight selections.
- The selections must be connected by a theme.
- Each concert must include between one and three new selections.

First Concert   Theme: _____

_____

_____

_____

Intermission

_____

_____

_____

Second Concert   Theme: _____

_____

_____

_____

Intermission

_____

_____

_____

Grammy Awards

SITUATION SETUP

The class becomes the board of directors for this year's Grammy Awards show. (You may wish to rename it "Student Choice Awards" or something similar.) Students do some of the work as a whole class and some in small groups determining categories, running the nominations, making and distributing the ballots, tallying the votes, and preparing a show that will highlight nominees and announce the winners.

GOAL

Students will discuss, listen to, and learn about a variety of songs, performers, and musical genres, past and present.

RULES

1. There are six basic "BEST" categories.
   - Female Musician
   - Male Musician
   - Ethnic Recording or Song
   - Newcomer or New Song
   - Classical Recording or Composition
   - Old-timer or Old Song

2. Students can add up to two more categories. (Discuss options.)

3. Student groups develop four nominees in each category.

4. Student groups develop, distribute, and tally voting ballots.

5. Students prepare a program for the award ceremony, including a brief description of each category.

6. Students present an awards program, including descriptions of each nominee, performances of some, and names of winners.

TEACHER DECISIONS

- How many students in each group?
- Which tasks will be done by groups and which as whole class?
- Who will be involved in voting? (class? grade? school? staff?)
- Will there be one big award program or one for each class?
- How will performances be done? (video? live? recorded? lip-synch?)
- Will students do a survey to gather ideas for nominations?
- Do you want students to write up project for local paper?

Name _____   Date _____

Simulation: Awards/Nominations

SITUATION

You are on the Board of Directors for this year's Grammy Awards. You are responsible for running the nominations, making and distributing the ballots, tallying the votes, and preparing the show, which will highlight nominees and announce the winners.

GUIDELINES

- There must be at least six "BEST" categories. (See below.)
- You may add no more than two categories.
- Each category must have four nominees.

NOMINEES

CATEGORY: *Best Female Musician*

_____

_____

CATEGORY: *Best Male Musician*

_____

_____

CATEGORY: *Best Newcomer or New Song*

_____

_____

CATEGORY: *Best Old-timer or Old Song*

_____

CATEGORY: *Best Ethnic Recording or Song*

_____

_____

CATEGORY: *Best Classical Recording or Composition*

_____

_____

CATEGORY: *(Your option)*

_____

_____

Name _____   Date _____

Simulation: Awards/Ceremony

DIRECTIONS

You are to make up the program for the awards ceremony.

GUIDELINES

- The program should include 10 nominated songs or performers.
- Each category will be described in a sentence or two.
- Nominees in each category will be read.
- Winners in each category will be announced.
- Each winner will be described in a sentence or two.
- Use the following draft to start. The final program should be done on separate paper complete with graphic designs.

TITLE: _____

Date: _____ Place: _____

Welcoming Remarks   by _____
   Performance of _____ **by** _____
      nominated for _____

First Category: _____
   Description: _____
   _____
   Nominees: _____
   _____
   Performance of _____ **by** _____
      nominated for _____

Second Category: _____
   Description: _____
   _____
   Nominees: _____
   _____

Closing Remarks   by _____

Simulation: Awards/MC's Notes

DIRECTIONS

You have been chosen to be one of the co-MCs for the awards ceremony. To be ready to make comments when the winner is announced, you need to prepare three to five sentences describing key facts about each nominee. Write in the category you have been assigned and the four nominees whose background description you are to prepare. Write in the descriptions of each.

CATEGORY _____

NOMINEES

1. _____

_____

_____

_____

2. _____

_____

_____

_____

3. _____

_____

_____

_____

4. _____

_____

_____

_____

Diversity Digest

SITUATION SETUP

A local publishing company is of the opinion that magazines today do not reflect the cultural diversity of our world. It is considering starting a new magazine, titled *Diversity Digest,* similar to *Reader's Digest.* It too would reprint articles from other magazines and write new articles to fill in the gaps. The company has hired your school to:

- see if today's magazines reflect our multicultural world.
- select and plan articles for the first issue.

GOAL

Students will discover the difficulty of finding true diversity in research and reading materials, discuss the reasons why, and explore the gaps by doing personal research in ignored areas.

SOME AREAS TO CONSIDER

Racial background, ethnic background, gender, age, economic status, subject matter

SOME EXTENSION POSSIBILITIES

Interdisciplinary

- Literature: Students actually research and write articles to fill the gaps.
- Other subjects: Have students include diversity of subject content as well.
- Have a local newspaper writer or editor come and talk about working for balance.

Mini-Publish

Actually print up copies of your *Diversity Digest.* (*Note:* If you do this, be sure to use only reviews or summaries of articles from other magazines due to copyright laws.)

Name _____ Date _____

Simulation: *Diversity Digest*/Search

Directions: (Each group member must do at least one report.)

- Search through a current news or entertainment magazine.
- Keep a tally of articles by topic (see below).
- Choose an article to be included in the premiere *Diversity Digest* issue. Include a brief summary. Explain why you recommend it.

Magazine Title: _____

Date and Issue: _____

TOPIC TALLY: Place a check for each article found. (Some articles may fit more than one category.)

	Mixture	Male	Female	Adult	Child
Caucasian					
Black					
Hispanic					
Oriental					
Native Peoples					

Recommended Article   Page(s): _____

Title: _____   Author: _____

Brief summary: _____

_____

_____

_____

Why you recommend it: _____

_____

_____

Name _____ Date _____

Simulation: *Diversity Digest*/Proposal

Directions

- Look over the descriptions of recommended articles and select some to be included in the premiere issue.
- Put together a proposed table of contents for the issue. List the title and a sentence describing each article.
- Check your proposal for gaps. Use the tally chart you used before.
- Star (*) articles that were recommended for reprinting.
- Circle the articles that will have to be written to fill gaps.

Table of Contents

Title: _____

Description: _____

_____

Title: _____

Description: _____

_____

Title: _____

Description: _____

_____

Title: _____

Description: _____

_____

Take a Stand!

SITUATION SETUP

The school has been asked to create a display to celebrate "Social Action Week" at the local City Hall. Music classes are to show songs that were written for or adopted by a social action cause. Working in groups, students create a display to demonstrate their song and its connection to and impact on the social issue.

SOME SONG POSSIBILITIES

"I Am Woman"—Helen Reddy (women's movement)

"We Shall Overcome" (civil rights)

"Abraham, Martin, and John" (lost leaders)

"Little Boxes"—Malvina Reynolds (suburban developments)

"New Math"—Tom Lehrer (math set theory)

"This Land Is Your Land"—Woody Guthrie

"We Are the World" (famine relief)

"Brother, Can You Spare a Dime?" (Depression era)

"Where Have All the Flowers Gone" (antiwar)

"Blowin' in the Wind"—Bob Dylan

"That's What Friends Are For" (AIDS project)

"99 Balloons" (antiwar)

"Janie's Got a Gun" (child abuse)

"Paradise by the Dashboard Light"—Meat Loaf (sexual pressure)

SOME EXTENSION POSSIBILITIES

- Interdisciplinary—project with the literature and art departments
- School exhibit of the display projects
- Performance: open exhibit with concert of some of the songs

Simulation: Take a Stand!

Directions

- Fill in your group's chosen song, its topic, and the project deadline.
- Write in which group member will be responsible for preparing each of the required elements. Check each off when completed.
- Write in who will get a copy of the song and/or recording. Check off when obtained and reviewed.
- Decide which optional visual elements to include and write who will be responsible for preparing them. Check off when completed.
- Hand this in with visual and written materials.

Song Title: _____

Song Topic: _____

Presentation Deadline: _____

Limits? _____

Required Written Elements

_____	_____	Composer and performer of song
_____	_____	Brief history of song, including when it was written
_____	_____	Brief explanation of why written
_____	_____	Brief summary of popularity
_____	_____	Brief description of public reaction
_____	_____	Explanation of impact on the issue

Required Aural Element

_____	_____	Listen to song

Optional Visual Elements

(You must include at least two.)

_____	_____	Picture of performer and/or composer
_____	_____	Graphics representing issue
_____	_____	Graphics representing reaction/impact
_____	_____	Recording illustrations
_____	_____	Copy of lyrics

John Philip Sousa

SITUATION SETUP

John Philip Sousa was offered a job playing in a circus band when he was just 13. Needless to say, he was excited by all he imagined a life with the circus would be. His parents learned of the offer. They were not pleased about their son joining the circus; they considered the circus an unsavory career. The next morning, June 9, 1868, his father told him to get dressed up and that they were going for a walk. The walk turned out to be to the Marine Recruiting Office, where Mr. Sousa enlisted John! (In those times parents could enlist a minor!) This was the beginning of John Philip Sousa's connection with the Marine Corps. Though originally signed up to apprentice as cabinetmaker, he spent his first four year enlistment as a "gofer" for the band (getting stands, sorting and filing music, doing errands, etc.). At his second enlistment he became a Principal Musician Third Class. Eventually he ended up leading the Marine Band. Under his direction it grew famous, touring nationally and internationally. At home the band played for the White House at such formal occasions as receptions, dinners, and dances. Sousa later formed his own internationally known band. He composed a great many marches for the band, some of which are recognized by thousands.

BACKGROUND RESOURCES

Marching Along, autobiography by John Philip Sousa, © 1928 Hale, Cushman & Flint.

The March King and His Band: The Story of John Philip Sousa, by Kenneth Berger, © 1957 Exposition Press, NY.

RECOMMENDED LISTENING

"Stars and Stripes Forever"
"Washington Post March"
"Semper Fidelis"

INTERESTING TRIVIA TO SHARE

- Sousa was 4'9" at first enlistment, 5'6$\frac{3}{4}$" at second.
- Sousa was a fastidious man who insisted on wearing a brand new pair of white gloves for each performance. That often meant packing hundreds of pairs for each international tour!

John Philip Sousa

BEFORE LESSON

Teacher Preparation

_____ Become familiar with story and the roles.

_____ Think through potential reactions of each character in case a student needs guidance.

_____ Copy and cut actors' role-play cards (page 81).

_____ Make name tags for each character to wear. These should be clear enough for class observers to read.

_____ Decide who you will ask to play each role.

_____ Decide if the role-play will be an introduction or follow-up.

_____ Decide if the focus will be Sousa or musical careers.

_____ Decide how many of the scenes you will be using.

_____ Decide if you are going to use written sheets or debrief the class orally.

Class Preparation or Follow-up

_____ Discuss or introduce historical importance of John Philip Sousa.

_____ Discuss Sousa's entry into his music career (see page 79).

_____ Listening lesson based on Sousa marches.

LESSON DAY

When Class Arrives

_____ Explain or review setting and premise.

_____ Explain or review rules. Announce signal for ending scene.

_____ Pass out roles and observer worksheet (page 82).

_____ Give actors three minutes to think while you pass out the role-play observer's worksheets to the rest of the class.

_____ Run the chosen scenes in order.

_____ Debrief the class using open discussion or worksheet (page 83).

_____ Collect worksheets if desired.

Optional Follow-up

_____ Assign "I Want to Be a Star!" worksheet on page 87 to be done individually or in groups.

_____ Role-play some parent/child discussions of different choices.

Role-play: John Philip Sousa/Roles

Mr. Sousa: Imagine you are Mr. Sousa. Why do you think you objected when you found out about John's circus band offer? What did you and your wife say in discussing the offer and deciding to enlist him in the Marines instead? How did you feel keeping the secret from John as you walked to the Marine Corps office? on the way home after enlisting him? two years later when John came for a visit? years later when you saw him perform at the White House?

Mrs. Sousa: Imagine you are Mrs. Sousa. What do you think you felt when you found out about John's circus band offer? What did you and your husband say in discussing the offer and deciding to enlist him in the Marines instead? How did you feel as John and your husband left for the Marine Corps office? How did you explain your decision to John afterward? How did you feel two years later when John came for a visit? years later when you saw him perform at the White House?

John Philip Sousa: Imagine you are John Philip Sousa. What did you feel when you got the circus band offer? What did you tell your best friend? your parents? How did you try to convince them that this was a great opportunity? How did you feel when you discovered they were enlisting you in the Marine Corps? What did you say to your best friend afterward? Two years later, what do you think you said to your parents? How did you feel when they saw you perform at the White House?

Role-play: John Philip Sousa/Observer

Directions: Write a phrase or two describing your reaction to what happened in each scene.

SCENE 1: John has just found out about the circus band offer. He is telling his best friend and talking about telling his parents.

_____

_____

SCENE 2: John has decided to tell his parents. In this scene, John tells them and they react.

_____

_____

SCENE 3: John's mother and father discuss what to do.

_____

_____

SCENE 4: Breakfast the next morning. The Sousas have made the decision to enlist John in the Marines, but John doesn't know.

_____

_____

SCENE 5: John and his father after leaving the Marine Corps office.

_____

_____

SCENE 6: John talking to his best friend after being signed up.

_____

_____

SCENE 7: It is two years later. John is home on leave and talking with his parents about the day he was signed up.

_____

_____

SCENE 8: John's parents have returned from a White House dinner at which John led the Marine Band. They are looking back over the decision to enlist him and what has happened since.

_____

_____

Role-play: John Philip Sousa/Debriefing

KNOWLEDGE: What exciting job offer did young John Philip Sousa receive?

_____

_____

COMPREHENSION: Tell why Sousa's parents thought they were doing the right thing for their son.

_____

_____

APPLICATION: How would you handle the situation if a son of yours presented you with similar news? (Remember that today you can't sign a minor into the Marines against his will.)

_____

_____

ANALYSIS: In what other ways could the Sousas have encouraged John's musical career?

_____

_____

SYNTHESIS: Imagine you are one of these people and answer the question. Circle the person and question you choose.

Mr. Sousa: How did you feel as you walked to the Marine Corps office? on the way home?

Mrs. Sousa: How did you feel after John and your husband left? How did you explain your decision to John afterward?

John Philip Sousa: How did you feel when you realized what your father did? What did you say to your parents?

_____

_____

EVALUATION: Explain why you think it was or was not a good decision for John's parents to sign him up for the Marines.

_____

_____

_____

_____

Women in Music

SITUATION SETUP

The local TV station is preparing a special for Women's History Month (March). They are going to have actors play the parts of a variety of women in music through the years. You have been chosen to be one of the actors. Each actor is responsible for researching her character and her history. The program format is an interview similar to other television newsmagazines, mixing interviews with the women themselves and comments from other people in their lives. Fortunately, the producers of the program have given you a list of topics that will be included. Working in groups, prepare by:

- researching the assigned role and preparing for the interview.

- choosing other people from or influenced by the woman's life to be included in the program, and preparing what they will say.

GOAL

Students will become aware of women in music they may not have encountered previously, the difficulties they met, and their successes and contributions.

SOME ROLE POSSIBILITIES (JUST A STARTER LIST)

Marian Anderson	Fanny Crosby (lyrics)	Helen Reddy
Marian McPartland	Jenny Lind	Josephine Baker
Joan Baez	Sarah Caldwell	Hildegard of Bingen
Ella Fitzgerald	Nannerl Mozart	Bette Midler
Clara Schumann	Linda Ronstadt	Wanda Landowski
Bonnie Raitt	Carole Bayer Sager	Diana Ross
Amy Grant	Phoebe Knapp (hymns)	Beverly Sills
Mildred and Patty Hill	Amy Beach	Maria Callas

EXTENSIONS

- Redo with other minority groups.

- Make it interdisciplinary with women from other fields.

- Have students write reaction papers.

Role-play: Women in Music

Part One: Research the person and write down points you want to use in the interview.

Name: _____

LIFE

Birth–Death: _____ Where lived: _____

Education: _____

_____

Significant events/facts: _____

_____

MUSICAL PROFILE

Training: _____

Musical field or genre (performer, composer, lyricist, etc.): _____

_____

Description and/or titles of work done: _____

_____

PROFESSIONAL DIFFICULTIES

_____

_____

OUTSTANDING CONTRIBUTIONS

_____

_____

_____

_____

OTHER?

_____

_____

_____

Part Two: On the back, write down other people in this person's life who might be good to include in the interview, and explain why.

I Want to Be a Star!

SITUATION SETUP

Each student has decided to follow a career in music or related to music. (Students will each choose a specific career.) Each student is to reflect on several specific careers and imagine the reaction of family and friends to their choice. (See the planning sheet on p. 87.)

- Students will be selected to role-play discussions with family and friends over specific choices.

- Students will discuss results and research several music or music-related careers.

GOAL

Students will discover the wide variety of music and music-related careers available. They will learn that not all require personal music performance skills. They will explore attributes of a variety of musical and music-related careers and their social and economic implications.

SOME CAREER POSSIBILITIES
(JUST A STARTER LIST)

piano tuner	instrument repair person
opera singer	disc jockey
recording technician	record store owner
piano teacher	drummer
restaurant pianist	orchestra musician
orchestra conductor	music librarian
chorus director	band director
recording manufacturer	music video director
record jacket designer	concert choreographer

THINGS TO CONSIDER

training required
personal musical skills/talent needed
interest factor
economic prospects
social implications

Role-play: I Want to Be a Star!/Plan

A. Name three to five kinds of jobs young musicians can get today.

_____

_____

_____

_____

_____

B. How might your parents react if you chose these music careers? Why?

1. drummer in a rock band _____

_____

2. school music teacher _____

_____

3. symphony orchestra player _____

_____

4. pop music singer _____

_____

5. pianist _____

_____

C. How would you convince your parents to encourage you in a music career? (You may choose any music career.)

_____

_____

_____

_____

_____

_____

_____

_____

_____

Role-play: I Want to be a Star!/Observer

Directions: As you watch each role-play, write down the career, list some benefits and drawbacks brought up, and tell whether you think the discussion was realistic or typical. Why or why not?

1st: Career: _____

Benefits/Drawbacks: _____

_____

Realistic discussion?: _____

_____

Comments: _____

2nd: Career: _____

Benefits/Drawbacks: _____

_____

Realistic discussion?: _____

_____

Comments: _____

3rd: Career: _____

Benefits/Drawbacks: _____

_____

Realistic discussion?: _____

_____

Comments: _____

4th: Career: _____

Benefits/Drawbacks: _____

_____

Realistic discussion?: _____

_____

Comments: _____

Role-play: I Want to Be a Star!/Follow-up

PART ONE

1. Name four jobs that require personal musical skill or talent.

   _____

   _____

2. Name four music-related jobs that don't.

   _____

   _____

3. Name four jobs that require personal musical knowledge but not necessarily performance talent or skill.

   _____

   _____

4. Name four music-related jobs that don't.

   _____

   _____

PART TWO

Choose any two music or music-related careers that you find intriguing. Do some research. Write a few sentences about each, describing its requirements, benefits, drawbacks, and implications. Continue on the back of the sheet if necessary.

1. _____

   _____

   _____

   _____

2. _____

   _____

   _____

   _____

Young People's Concerts

SITUATION SETUP

The local symphony orchestra has fallen on hard financial times and the governing board is reexamining the budget. For the last several years the orchestra has staged Young People's Concerts for area schoolchildren at a nominal fee. Area music teachers bring whole grade levels to these performances on field trips, supported by school board money or parent payment. These concerts usually feature a mix of classical music, light classics, and some familiar music such as movie themes. You are participating in an open meeting of the city council with the symphony board. The purpose of the meeting is to decide if youth concerts will continue. The issue is whether the value of the symphony youth concerts is worth the cost.

POSSIBLE ROLES

Elementary and/or high school music teachers

Local choir director

Symphony conductor

President, symphony board of directors

Elementary and/or high school students

Ladysmith Black Mambazo, male vocal group from South Africa

John Williams, conductor and composer, known for music for movies such as *Star Wars* and *Superman*

Billy Joel, composer and performer (middle-of-the-road pop)

Gloria Estefan, singer, dancer, drummer (rock)

Garth Brooks, composer and performer (crossover country music)

Bonnie Raitt, composer and performer (country, winner of several Grammy Awards)

Andrew Lloyd Webber, Broadway composer (*Jesus Christ Superstar*, *Phantom of the Opera*, and others)

Melissa Etheridge, composer/performer of current Top 10 hit song

Role-play: Concerts/Debater

Before the Debate: Write down your assigned role

_____

Are you going to argue **for** or **against** continuing Young People's Concerts?
_____ Is this your choice, or were you assigned to this position?

_____

List and explain three of the strongest reasons for that view:

1. _____

_____

_____

2. _____

_____

_____

3. _____

_____

_____

Find and write down a quote (a famous quote or a quote from a famous person)
that would help support that view:

4. _____

_____

_____

List two ideas for possible compromises you could offer:

5. _____

_____

_____

6. _____

_____

_____

Role-play: Concerts/Observer

During the Debate: Take notes of the best points made by each side to help you decide how you would vote. If possible, also jot down the initials or name of the person making the point.

FOR	AGAINST

Explain what compromise(s) you could support. Why?

_____

_____

_____

_____

_____

_____

Explain how you would vote. Why?

_____

_____

_____

_____

_____

_____

More Role-play and Simulation Ideas

Now that you have tried some of the simulations and have discovered how well they succeed, you are sure to want some more. Here is a list of idea starters you can take off and run with. You can use the format of any of the fully done simulations and do them with or without written follow-up.

Repertoire simulations usually work best in small groups or done as a teacher-led full class. They require at least 20 minutes of class time, depending on how much detail you plan to involve or whether you use them as discussion starters. Career or issue and history role-plays are very flexible. They can be done in mini-form (5 to 10 minutes) to introduce or tie up a lesson, as full class periods, or expanded to an interdisciplinary level in some cases.

Experiment with simulation ideas of your own, based on your curriculum specifics. Consider letting your students propose a role-play simulation. They can come up with wonderful ideas! Most important: Try some, then enjoy!

REPERTOIRE SIMULATIONS

1. Generate a list for a songfest at a retirement home.

2. Generate a list for a sing-along for kids under 8.

3. Generate a list for a mixed ages sing-along.

4. Generate a program list for one or more Young People's Concerts.

5. Generate a selection list for a relaxation tape.

6. Generate a selection list for an energizing tape.

7. Generate an hour radio show tracing the history of rock and roll.

8. Generate an hour radio show tracing the history of Broadway.

9. Generate an hour radio show introducing young people to opera.

10. Generate an hour radio show introducing young people to classical music.

11. Generate an hour radio show introducing members of the "older generation" to the pop music of young people (rap, heavy metal, rock).

12. Generate an hour radio show using the pop and classical music used in television and movies.

CAREER ROLE-PLAYS

1. Role-play Mozart's family when he was a child. Explore the feelings and pressures of a performance lifestyle on family members.

2. Role-play a current musician the same way (e.g., Michael Jackson, who started as a child with a family group and then went on his own, or someone else contemporary).

3. Compare and contrast Mozart and Michael Jackson. Explore how your students would feel in the place of one of these people.

4. Role-play the reactions of a variety of people when Beethoven was going deaf (an audience member, a close friend, Beethoven himself, an employer, etc.). Role-play their behavior before they realize what the problem is, and after.

5. Role-play a series of discussions concerning the fact that Tchaikovsky did not approve of his son being a composer and forced him into a bank job (Peter, his father, his boss, his coworkers, his friends, etc.). Role-play before the job, during the job, and after he leaves the job.

6. Role-play the reactions of a variety of people to George Gershwin's work that combined symphonic, classical style with jazz rhythms and stylings (audience members, concert promoter, Gershwin, leading musicians and composers of his era).

7. Role-play a quick series of job interviews between musicians and employers, to let students recognize the different requirements and responsibilities of a wide variety of music and music-related jobs (piano tuner, record store salesperson, newspaper music critic, recording studio sound technician, rock band drummer, etc.).

8. Role-play a job interview between musician and employer "Then and Now" to show how jobs have changed from 1750 to the present (music teacher, church organist) or more recent past to the present (radio disc jockey, pop music star).

9. Role-play a representative of an instrument company trying to introduce young people to the instruments and recruit them to learn to play one.

ISSUES AND HISTORY ROLE-PLAYS

1. Role-play family members/citizens/disc jockeys/musicians on the issue of censorship in music.

2. Role-play different generations debating "quality" music.

3. Role-play on this issue: Does music divide or unite people?

4. Role-play family members in conflict over a rock concert.

5. Role-play peers who prefer different music styles (country, rap, R & R, heavy metal, etc.).

6. Role-play a discussion between Joan Baez, her manager, her record producer, and her concert host about whether she should sing her war protest songs on her tour.

7. Role-play a panel discussion with Elton John ("Bennie & the Jets"), Paul McCartney ("Lucy in the Sky with Diamonds"), and Peter, Paul, and Mary ("Puff, the Magic Dragon") about whether there are hidden meanings in lyrics or whether people exaggerate that issue.

8. Role-play the occasion when President Abraham Lincoln had his band play the Confederacy's "hymn," "Dixie," at the signing of the treaty when the South surrendered (sympathetic, rubbing it in, appeasing, etc.).

9. Role-play the reactions and discussions when Benny Goodman took the step of including black musicians in his band. (Don't forget housing problems, concert admission, etc.)

10. Role-play several events with Ed Sullivan: his impact on early rock and roll, and the reactions of audience and network (e.g., proposing and hosting Elvis Presley, the furor over Elvis's hip gyrations, Ed's introduction of the Beatles to America, his insistence on censoring the lyrics to "Satisfaction" just before the Rolling Stones were to go on the air live).

11. Role-play the U.S. Postal Service committee's discussion over whether they should have an Elvis Presley stamp or not. (Historical impact of Elvis on music, appropriate role model?, etc.)

12. Role-play a school board discussion between teachers, students, board members, and community members about balancing sacred and secular music in school classes and concerts.

13. Role-play a panel discussion of possible ratings for records.

14. Role-play a panel discussion of censoring artwork, photos, and lyrics on album covers.

15. Role-play a quick series between parents and children disagreeing over dancing when various new dance styles began (waltz, Charleston, shimmy, jitterbug, 1960's crazes, disco, hip-hop, etc.).

INTERDISCIPLINARY UNITS

Many schools now have interdisciplinary activities as a routine part of their teaching. Some even have large "theme" weeks when regular content and books are put aside to delve into one topic with a total approach.

This chapter includes full materials for two possible units: "National Anthem Debate," with the primary focus on historical and musical issues and attitudes; and "World Cultural Hall of Fame," which is totally flexible, wide open to any and all subject areas and time periods. For these units, there are teacher guidelines, background material, possible roles, student worksheets, teacher checklists, hints for involving the entire school or community, and even a press release. These can be done as full-scale units or can be reduced for use by a single teacher or class.

Also included are full-page overviews for two other possible expandable interdisciplinary themes. "Evolution" uses skills from several subject areas, but the topic is music-based. "Space Probe" is a more general topic and can be expanded for as many subjects as desired.

Listed with the possible extensions for many of the other lessons and models in this book are even more interdisciplinary adaptions.

Teacher Guidelines

1. Contact colleagues well in advance.

2. Be sure that colleagues have a voice in the major decisions about the unit.

3. Invite them to join in the planning, but don't expect them to be as excited as you are.

4. Start small. It is much easier to expand once something is going well than to cut it back once it starts wobbling.

5. Don't panic. During every moment spent on these projects, the students are learning. Isn't that the main idea? Think *process*.

National Anthem Debate

BEFORE DEBATE

Teacher Preparation

_____ Become familiar with the situation setup, story, and roles.

_____ Decide which extensions you may include.

_____ Arrange for videotaping.

_____ Contact local newspaper/video channel. See sample press release on page 104. Adapt to fit your specific plan.

_____ Let parents/community know about the project (parent newsletter).

_____ Think of arguments for each character in case students need help.

_____ Cut role descriptions out, glue to index cards, and laminate if desired.

_____ Make name cards for each character to go on desks. (It is critical that these be large and clear enough to read from anywhere in the room.)

Class Preparation

_____ Discuss or introduce historical origin of "The Star-Spangled Banner."

_____ Discuss or introduce background of national anthem controversy.

_____ *Optional:* Explain the setting and rules for debate day.

_____ *Optional:* Brainstorm/discuss/learn alternative songs—before as introduction and preparation, or after as follow-up and extension.

_____ *Optional:* Do home or community survey of national anthem issue opinions. (Sample survey and thank-yous are on pp. 100 and 101.)

DEBATE DAY

Before Class

_____ Arrange chairs/desks.

_____ Have worksheets, role cards, and clock available.

_____ Set up video equipment.

When Class Arrives

_____ Explain or review setting and premise.

_____ Explain or review rules.

_____ Pass out roles and worksheets.

_____ Give class three minutes to think and write three main points. During this time, post the name cards.

_____ Run the debate.

_____ Give class three minutes at the end to finish worksheet and to vote. Remind them that assigned sides may change position.

_____ Collect worksheets.

_____ Tally votes.

_____ Announce vote.

Anthem/Preparation Materials

WHAT IS A "GOOD" NATIONAL ANTHEM?

Lyric content: What should it be?

A description of the country? its goals? its history? etc.

Is the sacred or secular nature of lyrics an issue?

Militaristic? inspirational? idealistic?

Vocabulary level: should small children be able to comprehend it?

Musical setting

Should it be by an American?

Should it be original?

What about its range or ease of singing?

What are the options?

What other songs could be considered?

("Grand Old Flag," "America the Beautiful," "America," "This Land Is Your Land," etc.)

How do they measure up to the standards discussed above?

POSSIBLE ROLES

(The basic 10 are marked •.)

Roles connected to the writing of "The Star-Spangled Banner"

• Francis Scott Key	John Skinner
• John Stafford Smith	Dr. Beanes
Samuel Sands	Judge Nicholson

Roles connected with the use of "The Star-Spangled Banner"

• President Woodrow Wilson

• U.S. Admiral Dewey

• President Herbert Hoover

Roles of present-day individuals

• School student	Local TV station reporter
• Elementary school music teacher	Local member of Congress
• American composer	Newspaper editor
• Marching band director	Immigrant from France
Historians (one for, • one against)	Member of U.S. Congress

For further explanation of these roles, look at the role description paragraphs on pp. 105–107.

EXTENSIONS

Interdisciplinary Connections

Writing: Students write about the national anthem controversy.
　　Editorials taking a side on the issue.
　　Journal entry about debate, staying in character assigned
　　Position paper on their personal opinion and reasons

Math: (works best if more than one class is involved in voting)
　　Using raw vote totals, tabulate:

- by class
- by grade
- by sex
- by student or teacher
- entire group

　　Work percentages for any or all of the above
　　Graph results

Social Studies: Explore how the political events and climate of different decades might affect how people would vote and why. Discuss the political climate and events that led to some of the other possible song choices. Explore national anthems of other countries and compare with their national philosophies.

Art: Posters or other graphic displays for each side or for alternative choice.

Computer: Create a database of possible song choices for national anthem and how they compare on the major issues.

Research Skills: Use *Readers' Guide to Periodical Literature* to locate articles on the issue at the time the song became the national anthem and since then.

Music Extensions

Expand to full Patriotic Music unit.

Have classes prepare commercials for alternative song choices.

Involve bands and/or choruses in demonstrating the anthem and options.

Extensions of Project Scope/Publicity

- Hold debate as a School Assembly, followed by school-wide vote. You could have each class coach several debate role-players.
- Videotape debate and air on local cable channel. You could even invite viewers to call or write in their votes.
- Alert local newspapers, television, and radio to project.
- Invite community members to attend debate and vote.
- Do as full school project, implementing and expanding the interdisciplinary options.
- Include in debate local people who have had to sing or lead "The Star Spangled Banner" at public events.

Anthem/Survey

Directions: Read questions, in order, to each volunteer. Write their responses in the blanks. Give them a thank-you slip.

Questions

1. What is the name of our current national anthem?
2. How long has it been our official national anthem?
3. Do you like or dislike "The Star-Spangled Banner"?
4. Why?
5. If the national anthem changed, what song would you choose?
6. Why?

Responses

An adult relative: Name _____ Approx. Age ____

_____

_____

_____

_____

_____

A student: Name _____ Age ____ Grade ____

_____

_____

_____

_____

_____

An adult in the community: Name _____

Occupation _____ Approx. Age ____

_____

_____

_____

_____

_____

_____

Anthem/Thank-you Notes

TO: National Anthem Survey Participants

Thank you for helping our school music students explore the way people feel about our national anthem. We believe it is very important for students to understand the power of music to express feelings. It is also important to discover the wide variety of personal musical preferences and how much individual reasons for those preferences can differ. This project lets our students explore these ideas while placing music in historical and human perspectives. Soon students will discuss the results of this survey, exploring "The Star-Spangled Banner" and other patriotic music. Finally, a debate that will feature students role-playing famous and not-so-famous individuals will be held. Voting and discussions will follow. If you are interested in more information, please call the school. Again, THANK YOU for helping with our project!

TO: National Anthem Survey Participants

Thank you for helping our school music students explore the way people feel about our national anthem. We believe it is very important for students to understand the power of music to express feelings. It is also important to discover the wide variety of personal musical preferences and how much individual reasons for those preferences can differ. This project lets our students explore these ideas while placing music in historical and human perspectives. Soon students will discuss the results of this survey, exploring "The Star-Spangled Banner" and other patriotic music. Finally, a debate that will feature students role-playing famous and not-so-famous individuals will be held. Voting and discussions will follow. If you are interested in more information, please call the school. Again, THANK YOU for helping with our project!

TO: National Anthem Survey Participants

Thank you for helping our school music students explore the way people feel about our national anthem. We believe it is very important for students to understand the power of music to express feelings. It is also important to discover the wide variety of personal musical preferences and how much individual reasons for those preferences can differ. This project lets our students explore these ideas while placing music in historical and human perspectives. Soon students will discuss the results of this survey, exploring "The Star-Spangled Banner" and other patriotic music. Finally, a debate that will feature students role-playing famous and not-so-famous individuals will be held. Voting and discussions will follow. If you are interested in more information, please call the school. Again, THANK YOU for helping with our project!

Name _____ Date _____

Anthem/Debater

"Should 'The Star-Spangled Banner' be our national anthem?"

Before the Debate: Read the card you were given. Think about the character you will play.

Name of Role _____
Notice whether or not you were given a starting position.
Stand on Issue (check one) _____For _____Against _____Undecided

Take a few minutes to think about what arguments or points you can use in the debate. Write down at least three points to use.

1. _____
2. _____
3. _____

During the Debate: Take notes here to help you decide how your character will vote at the end of the debate.

_____
_____
_____
_____

After the Debate: Take a few minutes to decide your vote. Think back, and write down here (or underline above) the argument that affected your decision the most.

_____
_____
_____
_____

Your Final Vote: (check one) _____ For _____ Against

Anthem/Observer

"Should 'The Star-Spangled Banner' be our national anthem?"

Before the Debate: Think about "The Star-Spangled Banner." If you were voting now on whether or not it should be our national anthem, would you vote: _____ For _____ Against _____ Undecided

Take a few minutes to think about your reasons. What points about "The Star-Spangled Banner" concern you most? List at least three reasons or issues.

1. _____
2. _____
3. _____

During the Debate: Take notes here to help you decide how you will vote at the end of the debate.

_____
_____
_____

After the Debate: Take a few minutes to decide your vote. Think back, and write down here (or underline above) the argument that affected your decision the most.

_____
_____
_____

Which side of the debate presented and supported their arguments better?

_____

What arguments or ideas would you give to the other side for the next time?

_____
_____

Your Final Vote: (check one) _____ For _____ Against

Anthem/Press Release

Students in the _____ school are taking part in a most unusual music and history project. They are exploring whether "The Star-Spangled Banner" should be our national anthem or not. Students have surveyed people throughout the community about how they feel toward our national anthem and whether they think it should be changed. They have studied how the song came to be written and how it became the national anthem. Other patriotic songs that could be alternatives to "The Star-Spangled Banner" have been studied and sung.

The culmination of this project comes _____ when the students will hold a debate. Students will role-play a variety of famous and not-so-famous individuals involved in a debate to "choose" a national anthem. At the close of the debate, participants and observers will vote and then discuss the results.

_____, the music teacher leading this project, believes it is very important for students to understand the power of music to express feelings. There is a wide variety of personal musical preferences and different individual reasons for those preferences. This project lets the students explore these ideas while placing music in historical and human perspectives. Anyone interested in more information may call the school.

FOR MORE INFORMATION CONTACT:

Anthem/Roles

These basic roles (1–10) and optional roles (11–22) can be cut and pasted to index cards to be used by the students playing each character. Feel free to add, adapt, or drop roles to fit your students.

1. You are Francis Scott Key, who wrote The SSB, and you are **for** The SSB as our national anthem. Be ready to explain why and defend your position.

2. You are President Woodrow Wilson, who first had The SSB used for official military occasions, and you are **for** The SSB as our national anthem. Be ready to explain why and defend your position.

3. You are U.S. Admiral Dewey, who first used The SSB for official Navy occasions, and you are **for** The SSB as our national anthem. Be ready to explain why and defend your position.

4. You are President Herbert Hoover. You are **for** The SSB as our national anthem and will sign the bill if it passes in Congress. You have not announced your position publicly but you may be pushed to announce it tonight. Be ready to explain why and defend your position.

5. You are an elementary school music teacher, and you are **against** The SSB as our national anthem. Be ready to explain why and defend your position.

6. You are an American composer, and you are **against** The SSB as our national anthem. You suggest "America the Beautiful." Be ready to explain why and defend your position.

7. You are a marching band director, and you are **against** The SSB as our national anthem. You suggest "Grand Old Flag." Be ready to explain why and defend your position.

8. You are a historian and a pacifist, and you are **against** The SSB as our national anthem. You suggest "America." Be ready to explain why and defend your position.

(continued)

9. You are John Stafford Smith, original composer of "To Anacreon in Heaven," the tune Key used for The SSB. We don't know your opinion yet. You decide and be ready to explain it.

10. You are John Skinner, the person who was with Key when he wrote The SSB. You are **for** The SSB as our national anthem. Be ready to explain why and defend your position.

11. You are a school student, and you represent all of the students who participated in a national poll. We don't know how the poll came out. You decide and be ready to explain and defend the student point of view.

12. You are a historian who has been campaigning very hard **against** The SSB as our national anthem. Be ready to explain why and defend your position.

13. You are Dr. Beanes, rescued by Key and Skinner, and you are **for** The SSB as our national anthem. Be ready to explain why and defend your position.

14. You are a congressman who has led the fight **against** The SSB as our national anthem. You have constituents who have suggested "America," "Grand Old Flag," "America the Beautiful," and "This Land Is Your Land." Be ready to explain and defend the one that you prefer.

15. You are a congressman and you are **for** The SSB as our national anthem. In fact, you are a sponsor of the bill to make it our national anthem. Be ready to explain why and defend your position.

16. You are an immigrant who came to America from France, and you are also a composer. We don't know your opinion. **You decide** and be ready to explain and defend it.

(continued)

Anthem/Roles *(continued)*

17. You are a historian who has been campaigning very hard **for** The SSB as our national anthem. Be ready to explain why and defend your position.

18. You are a reporter for the local television station. You have not announced your opinion and will listen to the debate until finally you are asked to state your opinion. Listen to the others and be **ready to decide** and defend your opinion.

19. You are Judge Nicholson, Key's brother-in-law, who first took The SSB to the printer. You are **for** The SSB as our national anthem. Be ready to explain why and defend your position.

20. You are the local member of Congress and are here at the meeting to find out how the people you represent want you to vote on the bill. Listen to the others and be **ready to decide** and defend your decision.

21. You are Samuel Sands, the young printer's helper who printed the first SSB flyers, and you are **for** The SSB as our national anthem. Be ready to explain why and defend your position.

22. You are the editor of a well-known newspaper, and you have not stated your opinion publicly, but have printed letters to the editor on both sides of the issue. **You decide** your opinion and be ready to explain it.

World Cultural Hall of Fame

BEFORE LESSON

Teacher Preparation

_____ Become familiar with the situation setup.

_____ Think through possible nominees in case students need advice.

_____ Find out if other departments will be involved. If so, meet with them to explain format and procedures.

_____ Decide what size the groups will be.

_____ Decide time frame for preparation and for nominations.

_____ Decide forum for nominations, depending on who is involved.

_____ *Optional:* Arrange for videotaping if desired.

_____ *Optional:* Contact local video channel and newspaper. (See sample press release on p. 116. Adapt to fit your specific plan.)

_____ *Optional:* Let parents/community know about project (newsletter).

Class Preparation

_____ Review some of the musicians previously studied.

_____ Explain hypothetical Hall of Fame.

_____ Explain the time limits for nominations and the deadlines.

_____ Hand out nomination and presentation sheets (pp. 113 and 114).

_____ *Optional:* Do home and community survey (pp. 111 and 112).

_____ *Optional:* Brainstorm ways to present nominees other than lecture or speech format (interviews about the nominee, film clips, etc.).

NOMINATION DAY

Before class

_____ Arrange chairs/desks with podium in front.

_____ Set up video equipment.

_____ Have overhead projector, easel, audio players available.

When class arrives

_____ Explain or review setting/premise.

_____ Run nominations.

_____ Explain or review rules.

_____ Give students time to circle their choices.

_____ Pass out observer worksheets (page 115).

_____ Collect worksheets.

FOLLOW-UP

_____ Count votes and announce inductees.

WHO DESERVES TO BE ELECTED?

Nominee's Attributes to Consider

- Performer? composer? both?
- Well-known personally?
- Broad musical audience?
- Difficulty of music?
- Training?
- Contributions to the development of music?

- Musical genre/style?
- Music well-known?
- Versatility?
- Groundbreaker?
- Skills in other fields?

Other Things to Think About

- Should the person's lifestyle be considered?
- Should financial success count?
- What other people could be considered?
- How do they measure up to the standards discussed above?

EXTENSIONS

- Prepare summary of life and achievements for nomination speech.
- Prepare audio presentation to accompany nomination.
- Involve bands and/or choruses in performing music of nominees.
- Journal entry about nomination as written by the nominee.
- Posters or graphics capturing highlights of nominee's achievements.

INTERDISCIPLINARY EXTENSION

Invite other subject areas to participate in the Hall of Fame by nominating people in their fields as well.

Those teachers should create similar attribute lists to consider. Use the same nomination approach. Decide whether there will be different categories for different fields or if there will be simply a set number of final inductees (for instance, the top 10 vote getters).

The primary learning is in preparing and giving the nomination presentations. Remember that and keep the assembly or voting low-key unless you are doing this for a large-scale school-wide project or community involvement.

PROJECT EXTENSIONS AND PUBLICITY

- Hold nominations at school assembly and take a school-wide vote.

- Have each class hold mini-nominations and vote to decide whom that class will nominate. Whole class works on presentation.

- Videotape nominations and air on local cable channel. Perhaps even invite viewers to call or write in their votes. (You could have ballot boxes in local business, ballots in local paper.)

- Alert local newspapers/television/radio to the project.

- Do as full school project, implementing and expanding the interdisciplinary options.

- Hold "Awards Show," complete with sealed envelopes to announce the winners. Videotape it, get coverage from newspaper, etc.

- Invite a local personality to be MC of the event.

Name _____ Date _____

Hall of Fame/Survey

Find three volunteers: adult relative, student, community adult

Explain project: "We are doing a school project studying famous people who have made outstanding contributions to the musical culture of the world. The idea is kind of an imaginary worldwide cultural Hall of Fame. We will be making nominations, giving speeches explaining the nomination, like the Academy Awards 'Lifetime Achievement' presentations, then voting. We would like you to help us come up with ideas for nominees."

Ask their opinions: 1. Who do you think was the most significant musician of the past and why? 2. Who do you think is the most significant musician of today and why? Write responses below.

RESPONSES:

An adult relative: Name _____ Approx. Age ____
Past _____
Why? _____
_____
Present _____
Why? _____
_____

A student: Name _____ Age ____ Grade ____
Past _____
Why? _____
_____
Present _____
Why? _____
_____

An adult in the community: Name _____
Past _____
Why? _____
_____
Present _____
Why? _____
_____

Hall of Fame/Thank-yous

TO: WORLD CULTURAL HALL OF FAME SURVEY PARTICIPANTS

Thank you for helping our school music students explore the way people feel about the people who have created the culture of our world. We believe that students need to understand the importance of culture in our lives. It is also important to discover the wide variety of people who have created our cultural heritage and diversity. This project lets our students explore these ideas and people. Soon students will discuss the results of this survey, choose whom they will nominate, and begin to prepare our nomination presentations. Finally, the nominations will be presented and followed up by discussions and voting. If you are interested in more information, please call the school. Again, THANK YOU for helping our project!

TO: WORLD CULTURAL HALL OF FAME SURVEY PARTICIPANTS

Thank you for helping our school music students explore the way people feel about the people who have created the culture of our world. We believe that students need to understand the importance of culture in our lives. It is also important to discover the wide variety of people who have created our cultural heritage and diversity. This project lets our students explore these ideas and people. Soon students will discuss the results of this survey, choose whom they will nominate, and begin to prepare our nomination presentations. Finally, the nominations will be presented and followed up by discussions and voting. If you are interested in more information, please call the school. Again, THANK YOU for helping our project!

TO: WORLD CULTURAL HALL OF FAME SURVEY PARTICIPANTS

Thank you for helping our school music students explore the way people feel about the people who have created the culture of our world. We believe that students need to understand the importance of culture in our lives. It is also important to discover the wide variety of people who have created our cultural heritage and diversity. This project lets our students explore these ideas and people. Soon students will discuss the results of this survey, choose whom they will nominate, and begin to prepare our nomination presentations. Finally, the nominations will be presented and followed up by discussions and voting. If you are interested in more information, please call the school. Again, THANK YOU for helping our project!

Hall of Fame/Nomination

"Who should be the first inductees?"

Step One: Think over the class discussion about how a person might deserve to be in a World Cultural Hall of Fame.

Performer? composer? both?   Musical genre/style?

Well known personally?   Music well known?

Broad musical audience?   Versatility?

Difficulty of music?   Groundbreaker?

Training?   Skills in other fields?

Contributions to the development of music?

Step Two: Choose the person your group will nominate.

Name _____

Step Three: Research this person and write down the points you want to include in your nomination presentation. Be sure you include information in each category.

Life: _____

_____

_____

_____

Musical Profile: _____

_____

_____

_____

Outstanding Contributions: _____

_____

_____

_____

Hall of Fame/Presentation

Directions

- Fill in the nominee your group has chosen and the time limits your teacher has given you.
- Decide which group member will be responsible for preparing each of the required elements. Check each off when completed.
- Decide what musical selections you will include, who will be responsible for preparing them, and check off when completed.
- Decide which optional visual element(s) you will include, who will be responsible for preparing them, and check off when completed.
- Decide what each group member will do in the presentation.
- Hand in this sheet, the planning guide, and the written presentation materials.

Nominee: _____

Presentation Length: _____ Deadline: _____

Required Written Elements:

_____ _____ Brief biographical summary

_____ _____ Brief summary of musical accomplishments

_____ _____ Explanation of outstanding contributions

Required Aural Element:

_____ _____ Sample(s) of person's music:

Optional Visual Elements: (You must include at least one.)

_____ _____ Picture of person

_____ _____ Graphic display representing achievements

_____ _____ Graphic display representing life highlights

_____ _____ Time line, map, or other visual

Presentation Responsibilities: (Each person must have one.)

_____

_____

Hall of Fame/Observer

"Who should be the first inductees?"

During the Nominations: Write the name of each nominee and take notes on what qualifies each for Hall of Fame induction.

lst Nominee _____

2nd Nominee _____

3rd Nominee _____

4th Nominee _____

5th Nominee _____

6th Nominee _____

Afterward: Think over presentations. Circle your choice. Hand in.

Hall of Fame/Press Release

Students in the _____ school are taking part in a most unusual project. They are exploring who would be nominated and inducted if there were a World Cultural Hall of Fame. Students have surveyed people throughout the community, asking who they feel should be nominated and why. They have discussed survey results and what kind of personal and professional attributes such a nominee should have. Groups of students each choose a nominee and prepare a nomination presentation similar to what is seen on "Lifetime Achievement" at the Academy Awards and Kennedy Center Honors. Nominations will be made in the categories of _____

_____.

The culmination of this project comes _____ when the students will hold a nomination ceremony. Student groups will present their nominees. Each group will attempt to show what outstanding contributions their nominee has made to the cultural richness and diversity of our world.

_____ , the teacher leading this project,

is assisted by colleagues _____.
The goals are to enable students to understand the importance of culture in our lives and to value the wide variety of people who have created our cultural heritage with their diverse gifts and skills. Anyone interested in more information may call the school.

FOR MORE INFORMATION CONTACT: _____

Further Interdisciplinary Units

MUSICAL EVOLUTION

Goal

Educated people work to understand the interdependence of different aspects of society. A musically educated person will want to understand how the musical instruments and folk songs of a country reflect the nature of that country's land, resources, and people.

Situation Setup

Imagine a long-lost continent with several countries. The people who lived on that continent thousands of years ago were forced to leave due to volcanic eruptions, plague, and earthquakes. Many came to the United States, bringing their folk songs with them. We've never known which songs and instruments came from which country because we knew so little about the continent. The recent discovery of a map (optional: and instrument drawings) has given musicologists the chance to discover how these songs and instruments evolved.

Skill Areas

Music, Social Studies, Science, Map Skills, Art

Student Project Elements (Work in groups.)

- Design a continent that might have created the songs listed. Include land forms, rivers, forests, mountains, canals, lakes, hot and cold climates, geography, natural resources, agriculture, oceans, rivers, logging, canal, etc., if appropriate.

- Draw a map of the continent with labels and key.

- Design and draw possible folk instruments that might have developed in such a place (instruments of dirt, gourds, horns, logs, bamboo, etc.).

Sample Song Possibilities

The Erie Canal	London Bridge
John Henry	A Capital Ship
Cockles and Mussels	Kookaburra
I've Been Working on the Railroad	Sourwood Mountain
She'll Be Comin' Round the Mountain	Drunken Sailor
Banana Boat Song (Day-O)	Marching to Pretoria

Follow-up

Discuss and analyze a real country or region and the logical evolution of songs and instruments (e.g., Africa, Maine, Ohio).

SPACE PROBE

Goal

Educated people work to understand that what they do and what they create represent their society and culture. They recognize that there are parts of any culture that inspire pride and parts that do not. Educated people are able to discuss and explain why they think each is each.

Situation Setup

A NASA space probe has just returned with a message inside. Scientists have just finished deciphering the message. It is from another human culture on a distant planet that asks us to send the probe back with artifacts and samples of our world culture. They will then decide if we are educated enough to contact further.

Areas

Any subject areas—the more inclusive the more realistic.

Student Project Elements (Work in groups.)

- Develop a proposal for the returning space probe.
- List the items you think should be included (maximum of 10).
- Be sure to include a balanced representation of all different elements of our culture and history.
- Be sure to include a balance of visual, aural, and written items.
- Write an explanation of why each should be included. (Use two to five sentences for each item.)

Class Follow-up

- Each group gives a copy of their proposal to other groups.
- Each group reviews all the proposals, combining and narrowing the list to a maximum of 15 items.
- Optional: The class then reviews those lists of 15 and after discussion comes up with a final list of 20 items.

Variations

1. Reverse it. You are on another planet and these are the things you have received in a space probe. What do they tell you about the culture?
2. Change it to the familiar "Time Capsule" idea. Make it for

   - 100 years in the future
   - to represent your state
   - to represent another state
   - to represent your country
   - to represent another country

Resource Materials

Here are a few odds and ends I hope will help make your work easier.

Curriculum Overviews

If your system requires formal lesson or unit plans or if you need to document the philosophical or educational base for these lessons, adapt these to match the specific unit content you are using.

Lesson Overviews

These give two examples of the same thing for specific lessons, one for a composer role-play and one for a game lesson.

Role-play Plan

Let students try their hands at setting up a role-play using this worksheet; or use it yourself until you get the knack of setting them up.

Measure Cards

Copy these, cut them out and mount them on cards to use with inductive lessons, concept attainment, or other applications. Do the same thing with instrument pictures and/or names of composers and their music, etc.

Activity Comparison Chart

As described on p. x, this is your handy reference to all of the full activities in this book, by categories. It should make your planning easier and save a lot of flipping and searching.

Children's Songs and Themes

A database of common children's songs by theme and form, this is great for the assembly simulation (p. 58), for concept attainment, and to use with your own inductive grouping lessons.

Symphonic Selections by Category

This database lets you get a head start on creating all kinds of groupings for simulations (pp. 65–69), concept attainment, inductive lessons, and more.

Curriculum Overviews

STYLES AND REPERTOIRE

Philosophical Base

Educated people discriminate and make choices based on knowledge and experience. The musically educated person will therefore learn to discriminate in musical choices, and will explore and value music as a means of expression and entertainment for a wide variety of situations.

Goal

Each student will use higher level thinking skills, their knowledge of music, and their personal experiences and opinions to evaluate and group various musical selections.

Objectives

Each student will:

- become aware of performance requirements of several typical performance situations (school assembly, symphony concert, radio show).
- explore how to use their personal musical experiences and knowledge to help evaluate and compare music choices.
- become aware of the variety of opinions and personal music preferences.
- become aware of how opinions and personal music preferences change among different people and over years.
- be able to explain their rationale for selections and groupings.

Activities

Working alone or in a group, each student will:

- explore a given category of musical repertoire.
- discuss and evaluate musical alternatives.
- select and plan musical selections for a given performance situation.

MUSICAL CAREERS

Philosophical Base

A musically educated person should be aware of the lives as well as the accomplishments of some of the leaders in the field and of lesser known musicians. Though some people are so instinctively talented they feel music chose them, educated people explore and choose careers based on knowledge, expectations, and experience.

Goal

Each student will gain a clearer, more realistic understanding of the lives of a variety of well-known musicians, community musicians, and the personal impact of a music career.

Objectives

Each student will:

- become familiar with specific events and accomplishments in the lives of various well-known musicians.
- become aware of the "real person" sides of famous composers by participating in simulations of real-life events and of emotional reactions connected to these events.
- become aware of a variety of today's careers in music and related to music.
- become aware of the use and effect of music in people's daily lives, regardless of their primary career choice.
- become aware of the negative reactions sometimes caused by the choice of a music career and possible reasons for them.

Activities

Each student will:

- explore experiences in the careers of well-known musicians.
- explore music in the personal and professional lives of people today.
- discuss music's impact on their emotional and professional lives.
- explore musicians' problems that seem to recur throughout history.

ISSUES AND HISTORY

Philosophical Base

Educated people have historical perspective, make choices based on knowledge and experience, and recognize the importance of outlets for emotion. The musically educated person will relate music to historical developments, learn to discriminate in musical choices, and will explore and value music as a means of expression for a person or society.

Goal

Each student will use higher-level thinking skills, their knowledge of music, and their personal experiences and opinions to evaluate specific controversial issues, both historically and in present-day music.

Objectives

Each student will:

- become aware of the basic viewpoints on specific issues in music history.
- become aware of the historical background of these issues.
- become aware of some of the arguments for and against various viewpoints on these issues.
- become aware of options and opinions, and their results.
- learn how to use the experiences of others and themselves to help compare and evaluate choices.
- become aware of the variety of opinions and personal music preferences.

Activities

Each student will:

- complete a community survey about a given issue and its history.
- explore and evaluate alternatives and choices in the controversy.
- be an observer or debater on the merits and results of differing views.
- make a personal decision on the issue and explain why.

ELEMENTS OF MUSIC

Philosophical Base

A musically educated person should be aware of the ingredients and attributes of music. Though people are capable of using and enjoying music without understanding its mechanics, educated people study and explore what goes into the music to gain a deeper knowledge and understanding.

Goal

Each student will gain a clearer, more accurate understanding of the components of music and their use.

Objectives

Each student will:

- become familiar with a variety of the traditional attributes of music: melody, harmony, rhythm, form, tone color.
- become familiar with the components of those elements and how they function to create music.
- be able to identify and label studied components accurately.
- be able to manipulate the components and elements of music.
- become aware of the historical background or development of the components and elements of music.

Activities

Each student will:

- explore various elements of music.
- manipulate the components of pitch and rhythm in melodies.
- explore and manipulate a variety of instrumental tone colors.
- explore and experience differences in harmonic combinations.
- explore and experience differences in form and ensemble.

NATIONAL ANTHEM DEBATE

Philosophical Base

Educated people have historical perspective, make choices based on knowledge and experience, and recognize the importance of outlets for emotion. The musically educated person will relate music to historical developments, learn to discriminate in their musical choices, and explore and value music as a means of expression for a person or society.

Goal

Each student will use higher level thinking skills, their knowledge of music, and their personal experiences and opinions to evaluate "The Star-Spangled Banner" as our national anthem.

Objectives

Each student will:

- become aware of "The Star-Spangled Banner"'s origins and history.
- become aware of arguments for and against it as our national anthem.
- become aware of patriotic music and songs that could potentially be national anthem alternatives.
- learn how to use their personal musical experiences to help evaluate and compare music choices.
- become aware of the variety of opinions and personal music preferences.

Activities

Each student will:

- complete a community survey about the national anthem.
- explore "The Star-Spangled Banner"'s origins, history, and controversy.
- explore and evaluate musical alternatives.
- be an observer or debater on the merits of "The Star-Spangled Banner" as our national anthem.
- make a personal decision on its value and be able to explain why.

Sample Lesson Overviews

JOHN PHILIP SOUSA ROLE-PLAY

Goal

Each student will use personal experiences and opinion to consider what it was like for John Philip Sousa to lose his first job opportunity and be forced into the Marines by his father.

Objectives

Each student will:

- become aware of John Philip Sousa's importance to American music.
- become aware of how John Philip Sousa began his music career.
- become aware of differences in parental rights since the 1800's.

Activities

Each student will:

- observe or participate in a series of role-play scenes from the life of John Philip Sousa.
- participate in a discussion of how his parents' choices affected the musical development and career of John Philip Sousa.
- participate in a discussion of how musical careers can be encouraged and pursued.

CAN YOU HUM A FEW BARS?

Goal

Each student will use personal experiences and knowledge to identify folk songs by their country of origin.

Objectives

Each student will:

- be able to hum the melody of a variety of folk songs, given the name of the song.
- be able to recognize the melody of a variety of folk songs on hearing.
- be able to match folk melodies with their country of origin.

Activity

Each student will:

- participate alternately as a hummer and a listener in an aural review game using folk melodies and countries studied during the unit.

Name _____ Date _____

Role-play Plan

Topic: _____

Main Character
Name: _____
Known for: _____
Age at the time of this situation: _____

Role-Play Situation (continue on back if needed)
Setting: _____
Background: _____
_____
Issue: _____
_____

Other Characters in the Scene (continue on back if needed)
Name: _____Relation to main character: _____
Importance: _____
Name: _____Relation to main character: _____
Importance: _____
Name: _____Relation to main character: _____
Importance: _____
Name: _____Relation to main character: _____
Importance: _____

Focus Questions for Observers (continue on back if needed)
1. _____
2. _____
3. _____

Debriefing Discussion Focus

_____
_____
_____

Measure Cards

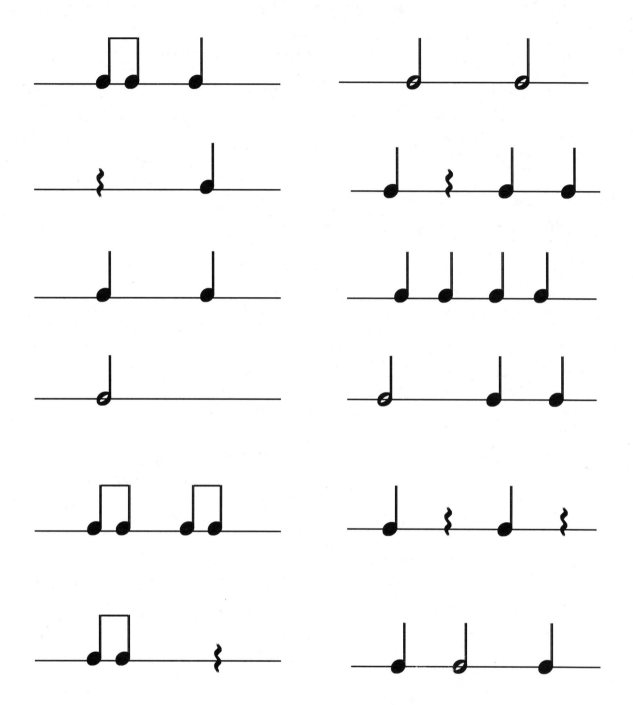

Measure Cards *(continued)*

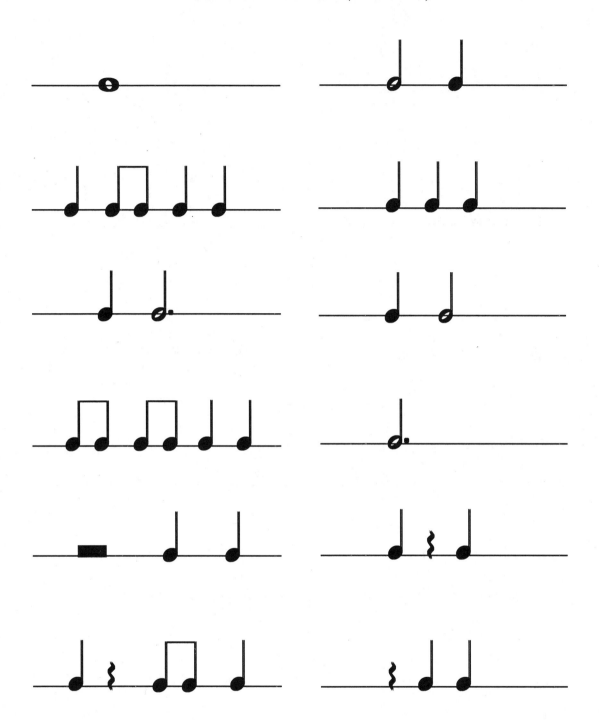

Measure Cards *(continued)*

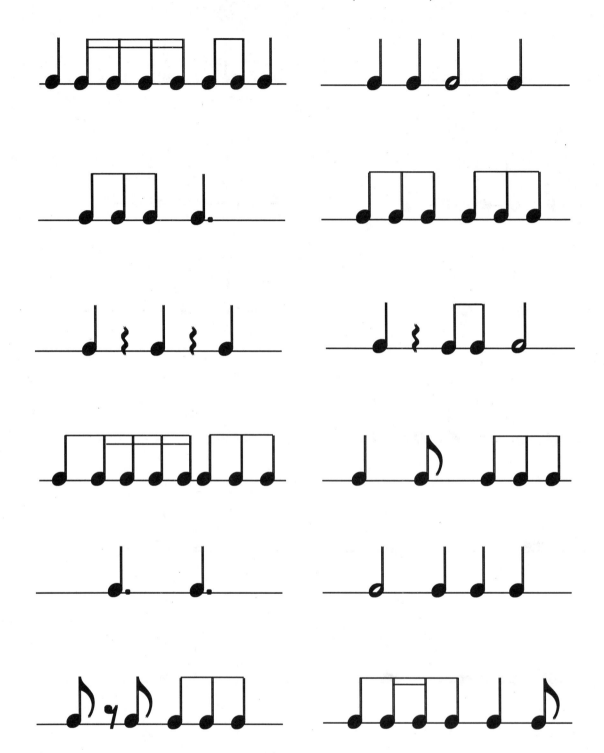

duple meter	2 beats
triple meter	4 beats
compound meter	3 beats
all sound	steady
all silence	syncopated
sound and silence	leftovers

Activity Comparison Chart

Lesson	Page	Format	PMSNR	Reper	Careers	Issues	History	Element	Interd	Comm
A Musical Week on the Town	7	Scavenger Hunt	xxxx		xxx					xxx
And Then What Happened?	43	Active				xxx	xxx			
And Venn Again . . .	38	Active		xxx		xxx	xxx			xxx
Around the World	12	Scavenger Hunt	xxxx	xxx		xxx				
Can You Hum a Few Bars?	40	Active and Noisy		xxx						
Children's Song Assembly	58	S: Group or Indiv		xxx	xxx					
Diversity Digest	74	S: Groups	xxxx			xxx	xxx		xxx	
Do You Know the Musical Staff?	5	Scavenger Hunt	xxxx		xxx	xxx	xxx			xxx
Evolution	117	S: Lg Unit		xxx					xxx	
Grammy Awards	70	S/RP: flexible	xxxx	xxx		xxx	xxx			
Hear Me Roar?	14	Scavenger Hunt	xxxx		xxx	xxx	xxx			xxx
I Want to Be a Star!	86	RP: flexible			xxx					
Instrument Families	49	Inductive						xxx		
Instrumental Charades	45	Active								
Instruments, Tone Color	52	Concept Attain						xxx		
"J.Q. Public" Speaks	18	Interview	xxxx	xxx						xxx
John Philip Sousa	79	RP: 3 basic roles	xxxx		xxx					
Library Music	22	Interview	xxxx							xxx
Move Over, Billboard!	6	Scavenger Hunt	xxxx							xxx
Music in Religion	24	Interview	xxxx	xxx	xxx		xxx			xxx
National Anthem Debate	97	S/RP: 10–25 rol	xxxx	xxx		xxx	xxx		xxx	xxx
Paper Ball Catch	41	Active	xxxx				xxx	xxx		xxx
Play It Again, Sam	21	Interview	xxxx							xxx

PMSNR = Personal Music Skill Not Required, Reper = Repertoire, Inter = Interdisciplinary, Comm = Community Involvement, S = Simulation, RP = Role-Play

(continued)

Activity Comparison Chart *(continued)*

Lesson	Page	Format	PMSNR	Reper	Careers	Issues	History	Element	Interd	Comm
Program Music	28	Concept Attain		xxx						
Radio Disc Jockey	23	Interview	xxxx							xxx
Read All About It	9	Scavenger Hunt	xxxx							xxx
Remember When?	19	Interview	xxxx	xxx			xxx			xxx
Repertoire (Song Classifications)	31	Concept Attain	xxxx	xxx						
Sing Out!	20	Interview	xxxx		xxx					xxx
Space Probe	118	S: Lg Unit		xxx			xxx		xxx	
Survey Says	13	Scavenger Hunt	xxxx	xxx						xxx
Symphony Board	66	S: Group	xxxx	xxx	xxx					
Symphony Conductor	68	S: Individual	xxxx	xxx	xxx					
Take a Stand!	78	S: Groups		xxx					xxx	
Tape Store Manager	25	Interview	xxxx		xxx					xxx
Time Signatures	51	Inductive						xxx		
Tone Color Groupings	52	Inductive						xxx		
Where Can I Find It?	10	Scavenger Hunt	xxxx							xxx
Who Am I?	37	Active			xxx	xxx	xxx			
Who's on the Line?	45	Active				xxx	xxx			
WKID Radio	62	S: Groups	xxxx	xxx	xxx	xxx	xxx			
Women in Music	85	RP: flexible			xxx	xxx	xxx		xxx	
World Cultural Hall of Fame	108	S: Lg Unit		xxx	xxx	xxx	xxx		xxx	xxx
Young People's Concerts	90	S/RP: flexible	xxx	xxx	xxx	xxx				xxx

PMSNR = Personal Music Skill Not Required, Reper = Repertoire, Inter = Interdisciplinary, Comm = Community Involvement, S = Simulation, RP = Role-Play

Children's Songs and Themes

Title	Country	Folk	Patriotic	Round	Seasonal	Disney	Action	Ocean	Movie	Pattern
Aladdin	USA	xxx				xxxxx			xxxx	
Alouette	France	xxx								xxxxx
America (My Country 'Tis)	USA		xxxxxx							
B-I-N-G-O	USA	xxx					xxxxx			xxxxx
Beauty and the Beast	USA					xxxxx			xxxxxx	
Clementine	USA	xxx								
Day-O (Banana Boat Song)	Jamaica	xxx								xxxxx
Drunken Sailor (What Shall We Do)	USA	xxx						xxxx		xxxxx
Frere Jacques	France	xxx		xxxx						
Frosty the Snowman	USA				xxxxxx					
Funiculi, Funicula	Italy	xxx								
Grand Old Flag (Cohan)	USA		xxxxxx							
Happy Birthday	USA				xxxxxx					
Hokey-Pokey	USA	xxx					xxxxx			xxxxx
I've Been Working . . . Railroad	USA	xxx								
If You're Happy and You Know It	USA	xxx					xxxxx			xxxxx
Itsy Bitsy Spider	USA	xxx					xxxxxx			
Jingle Bells	USA				xxxxxx					
Kookaburra	Australia	xxx		xxxx						
Kum Ba Yah	Africa	xxx								
Little Bunny Foo-Foo	USA	xxx					xxxxx			xxxxx
London Bridge	England	xxx					xxxxx			
Marching to Pretoria	AfriCa	xxx								
My Bonnie Lies Over the Ocean	USA	xxx					xxxxx	xxx		
Row, Row, Row Your Boat	USA	xxx		xxxx				xxx		

(continued)

132   *Creative Activities for Music and Humanities Classes*

Children's Songs and Themes *(continued)*

Title	Country	Folk	Patriotic	Round	Seasonal	Disney	Action	Ocean	Movie	Pattern
Rueben and Rachel	USA	xxx								xxxxx
She'll Be Comin' . . . Mountain	USA	xxx								xxxxx
Somewhere Out There	USA					xxxxx			xxxx	
Star-Spangled Banner	USA		xxxxxx							
Supercalifragilisticexpialidocious	USA								xxxx	
This Land Is Your Land (Guthrie)	USA		xxxxxx							
Three Blind Mice	USA	xxx		xxxx						
Twinkle/ABCD/Baa . . . Black Sheep	Classical	xxx								xxxxx
Waltzing Matilda	Australia	xxx								
White Coral Bells	England	xxx		xxxx						
Whole World in His Hands	Spiritual	xxx								xxxxx
Yankee Doodle	USA	xxx	xxxxxx							
Yankee Doodle Dandy (Cohan)	USA		xxxxxx						xxxx	
Zip-a-dee-doo-dah	USA					xxxxx			xxxx	

Symphonic Selections by Category

Title	Composer	Nationality	Period	Ge	Pa	Mo	Se	Pr	Da	An	Op
Afternoon of a Faun	Debussy	France	Modern								
An American in Paris	Gershwin	USA	Modern	x							
Blue Danube Waltz	Strauss	Austria	Romantic	x							
Bolero	Ravel	France	Modern								
Carmen	Bizet	France	Romantic								x
Carnival of the Animals	Debussy	France	Modern							x	
Danse Macabre	Saint-Saëns	France	Romantic			x	x	x			
E.T., Theme from	Williams	USA	Contemporary			x					
El Salon Mexico	Copland	USA	Contemporary	x							
Finlandia	Sibelius	Finland	Modern	x	x						
Firebird Suite, The	Stravinsky	Russia	Modern					x		x	
Flight of the Bumblebee	Rimsky-Korakov	Russia	Romantic							x	
Four Seasons, The	Vivaldi	Italty	Baroque				x				
Grand Canyon Suite	Grofe	USA	Modern	x				x			
Hallelujah Chorus (Messiah)	Handel	England	Baroque				x				
Hungarian Dances	Brahms	Germany	Romantic	x					x		
Jesu, Joy of Man's Desiring	Bach	Germany	Baroque								
Lincoln Portrait	Copland	USA	Contemporary		x		?				
London Symphony	Haydn	Austria	Classical	x							
Magic Flute, The	Mozart	Austria	Classical								x
Messiah, The	Handel	England	Baroque				x	x			
Night on Bald Mountain	Mussorgsky	Russia	Romantic					x			
Ninth Symphony	Beethoven	Germany	Classical								

Ge = Geographic, Pa = Patriotic, Mo = Movie, Se = Seasonal, Pr = Program, Da = Dance, An = Animals,
Op = Opera

(continued)

Symphonic Selections by Category (continued)

Title	Composer	Nationality	Period	Ge	Pa	Mo	Se	Pr	Da	An	Op
Nutcracker Suite, The	Tchaikovksy	Russia	Romantic				x	x	x		
Peer Gynt Suite	Grieg	Norway	Romantic					x	x		
Peter and the Wolf	Prokofiev	Russia	Modern					x		x	
Pictures at an Exhibition	Mussorgsky	Russia	Romantic					x			
Polonaise	Chopin	Poland	Romantic						x		
Rhapsody in Blue	Gershwin	USA	Modern								
Sabre Dance	Khatchaturian	Armenia	Modern					x	x		
Scheherazade	Rimksy-Korsakov	Russia	Romantic					x			
Sleigh Ride	Anderson	USA	Contemporary				x	x			
Sorcerer's Apprentice, The	Dukas	France	Romantic				x	x			
Star Wars, Theme from	Williams	USA	Contemporary			x					
Star and Stripes Forever	Sousa	USA	Modern		x						
Superman, Theme from	Williams	USA	Contemporary			x					
Surprise Symphony	Haydn	Austria	Classical								
Turkish March	Mozart	Austria	Classical	x							
Unfinished Symphony	Schubert	Austria	Romantic								
Unsquare Dance, The	Brubeck	USA	Modern						x		
Variations on "America"	Ives	USA	Modern		x						
Walk to the Bunkhouse (Red Pony Ste)	Copland	USA	Modern	?						?	
Washington Post March	Sousa	USA	Modern	x							
Water Music	Handel	England	Baroque	?							
William Tell Overture	Rossini	France	Romantic					x			x

Ge = Geographic, Pa = Patriotic, Mo = Movie, Se = Seasonal, Pr = Program, Da = Dance, An = Animals, Op = Opera

Creative Activities for Music and Humanities Classes